Louis Jac

The Original 1985 Courtroom Testimony in the Trial of Agudas Chasidei Chabad vs. Rabbi Sholom Dovber (Barry) Gourary

Editors:

Menachem Butler and Ivor Jacobs

Published in Honor of 5 Tevet 5782

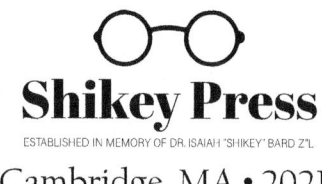

Cambridge, MA • 2021

The Original 1985 Courtroom Testimony in the Trial of
Agudas Chasidei Chabad vs. Rabbi Sholom Dovber (Barry) Gourary

Louis Jacobs, author

Menachem Butler and Ivor Jacobs, editors

Cover photo courtesy of Rikki Gordon Lewin.

© 2021, All Rights Reserved

ISBN: 979-8-9852681-9-5

Published by Shikey Press
Cambridge, MA

www.ShikeyPress.com
info@ShikeyPress.com
Twitter @ShikeyPress

Table of Contents

5 Tevet 5782
December 9, 2021

Preface by Menachem Butler i

Foreword by Nathan Lewin v

Introduction by Ivor Jacobs vii

Courtroom Testimony by Louis Jacobs 1

PREFACE

Menachem Butler

5 Tevet 5782
December 9, 2021

On the contemporary Chabad-Lubavitch calendar, there seems to be no day that is filled with greater joy and serenity than The Fifth Day of Tevet, "a Festival of the Books." This day of "Didan Notzach!" was declared in the late 1980s as a "new Yom Tov" and within it the festivity of recalling the happiness felt by the Lubavitcher Rebbe following the secular court ruling by a non-Jewish judge that the library, which had been rescued from Europe by the Lubavitcher Rebbe's father-in-law and predecessor as spiritual leader of the movement, belonged to the Chabad-Lubavitch movement as a whole. A federal court in New York ruled that the contents of the Library of Agudas Chasidei Chabad would not be transferable to other members of The Previous Lubavitcher Rebbe's family, particularly to his grandson (and nephew of The Lubavitcher Rebbe), Rabbi Sholom Dovber (Barry) Gourary.

This small volume, published by Shikey Press on The Fifth of Tevet in 5782 (2021) is not the place for the history and full analysis of the legal proceedings of this court case, or even to measure its impact within the Chabad-Lubavitch movement. For those interested, a modest-sized monograph, compiled by Rabbi Moshe Bogomilsky and first published

i

in 2006, and frequently reprinted, is entitled: *Hei Teves, Didan Notzach: The Victory of the Seforim - A Synopsis of Events Related to the Retrieval of Seforim, the Court Battle, the Legal Decisions and the Rebbe's Perspective*, recalls the narrative from the (victorious) side of the Lubavitcher Rebbe and the international community of Chabad-Lubavitch. (Additionally published booklets and websites aligned with the Chabad-Lubavitch movement are likewise filled with related and relevant materials.) To date, however, the perspective of Rabbi Sholom Dovber (Barry) Gourary has not been publicly offered. Furthermore, the many thousands of pages of testimony and supporting legal documentation, which presented nuanced intricacies of the Chabad-Lubavitch history within the context of this overall episode, and more, are likewise not publicly available. Legal scholars and academic researchers of various disciplines have occasionally made use of these documents within their research and scholarly writings. However, a full (and impartial) analysis of the legal issues surrounding the Library of the Agudas Chasidei Chabad remains a scholarly desideratum. Only with the complete accessibility to the primary text court documents, as well as with supporting interviews and related ephemera, can a full study of this entire episode even be possible. It is my opinion that the academic study of these documents and analysis would have to occur in an impartial setting, not attached with the Chabad-Lubavitch movement.

Indeed, one of the witnesses who testified in this case was Rabbi Dr. Louis Jacobs of London, England, who was serving as a visiting professor at Harvard Divinity School from 1985 to 1986. For those who wish to read more of the context of just how significant it was for Rabbi Jacobs to be called as a witness for The Lubavitcher Rebbe, see the recently-published biography by Harry Freedman, *Reason To Believe: The Controversial Life of Rabbi Louis Jacobs* (2020), and its focused discussion of "The Lubavitch Trial," pp. 212-215.

It is against this backdrop that Shikey Press is honored to offer this "fascinating trial fragment," as described by Mr. Nathan Lewin in the Foreword to this volume. Mr. Lewin -- a scion of a prominent Polish rabbinic family of communal activists (and full disclosure: a mentor and friend of this author) -- is not a Chasid, and, in fact, The Lubavitcher Rebbe insisted to his chasidim during the trial that they should allow him to focus on his legal efforts in the case and not try to make him into a Chasid! Mr. Lewin served as The Lubavitcher Rebbe's attorney and represented his interests during all of the matters surrounding the Library of the Agudas Chasidei Chabad. We are most appreciative that Mr. Lewin shared these brief reflections in the Foreword to this volume. As well, we are thankful to Mrs. Rikki Gordon Lewin for allowing us to reproduce the cover photo that she took as her husband, Mr. Nathan Lewin, was carried on the shoulders of Chabad-Lubavitch chasidim into the main sanctuary of Chabad World Headquarters at 770 Eastern Parkway, following the legal victory in 1987.

Shikey Press is also grateful to the friendship of Mr. Ivor Jacobs of London, both for his assistance in making available the contents of his father's courtroom testimony, for offering his brief Introductory reflections, and for serving as co-editor of this volume. May he and his family continue to honor their father's memory in their patronage and support of the UK-based charity, Friends of LouisJacobs.org.

One final point. The text that is reproduced in this volume is the court stenographer's transcription of the testimony. At times, corrections were made on the document, though there are still some mistranscriptions that remain in the text. For example, as noted to me in a private email communication by Professor David Berger (and shared here with his permission), "in Louis Jacobs' testimony, there is a passage where he is reported to have used the word pantheism several times when he almost certainly said panentheism. Later on, there is one instance where the transcript reads 'pan' followed by two letters covered by black ink and unreadable followed by 'theism'. There the original transcriber correctly wrote 'panentheism' and someone 'corrected' it."

Finally, on the first anniversary following the victorious ruling in federal court, the Lubavitcher Rebbe issued a directive on The Fifth of Tevet of 5749 to his followers and supporters of the Chabad-Lubavitch Movement that observance of the occasion of The Fifth of Tevet is to be fulfilled by increasing the times of personal Torah study, as well as building personal book collections and expanding the efforts of Jewish libraries in general, with a particular focus on the Library of Agudas Chasidei Chabad. Though I do not know if the publication of this volume would be considered as part of The Lubavitcher Rebbe's 5749 instruction, reading through the testimony of Rabbi Dr. Louis Jacobs, the reader will see first-hand of the crucial role that a non-Chabad rabbi and scholar had in bringing about the victorious result of Didan Notzach!

Menachem Butler
Cambridge, MA

Menachem Butler is the Program Fellow for Jewish Legal Studies at the Julis-Rabinowitz Program on Jewish and Israeli Law at Harvard Law School. He is an Editor at Tablet Magazine, a Co-Editor at The Seforim Blog, and Founder and Co-Publisher of Shikey Press. He lives in Cambridge, MA.

FOREWORD

Nathan Lewin

5 Tevet 5782
December 9, 2021

Rereading Rabbi Louis Jacobs' testimony today reminds me how blessed our trial team was by the confidence that the Lubavitcher Rebbe vested in us. We knew that Rabbi Jacobs was controversial from a religious aspect, but we also knew that both because of his formidable scholarship and his impressive academic credentials his testimony would affect Judge Charles P. Sifton's judgment and would be very helpful. Jerry Shestack did a phenomenal job in preparing Jacobs' testimony and leading him through it. Jacobs' review of Chassidus and Chabad philosophy was instructive and interesting to Judge Sifton, who we knew had been the son-in-law of the famous theologian Reinhold Niebuhr. Since Jacobs was teaching that year at Harvard's Divinity School, he was available to testify and expressed support for our legal position. We knew that if his rejection in the UK was raised on cross-examination as it was, tribute to his excellence was acknowledged by his critics.

Shikey Press appropriately publishes this fascinating trial fragment on the Fifth of Tevet, the date celebrated by the Chabad-Lubavitch movement worldwide as *"Didan Notzach"* to commemorate the court victory. The Rebbe instructed that it be a day for studying and building up a library of seforim for adults and children. In the spirit of Chanukah — the holiday it so closely follows— may it always be a day of joy for *"oskei torasecha"* — those who occupy themselves with the lessons of Torah.

May we merit each day to grow in wisdom and to share the light and love of learning that this case has come to represent.

Nathan Lewin is a Washington-based lawyer who successfully represented Agudas Chasidei Chabad in a federal lawsuit over ownership of the library collected by the Sixth Lubavitcher Rebbe.

INTRODUCTION

Ivor Jacobs

5 Tevet 5782
December 9, 2021

There is much about this court case that deserves reflection and indeed honoring and it is wonderful that this book has been brought to light by Shikey Press and bringing this remarkable episode to a wider audience.

It is certainly testament to the Lubavitcher Rebbe's openness that he should have reached across the religious divide to Rabbi Dr Louis Jacobs as one of the prosecution's key witnesses. Rabbi Jacobs was an expert in the history of the movement but his name had been tarnished throughout the Orthodox world in the years following his publication of the now infamous We Have Reason To Believe which gave rise to The Jacobs Affair in the UK. This episode was even referenced during his witness cross-examination by the defence, in an attempt to cast doubt on his scholarly opinion in support of the Rebbe's position. It is certainly extraordinary that of the many Chabad houses that we have been to, Rabbi Jacobs to this day is held in the highest regard given his prominence in the case. He even had representatives from Chabad headquarters in New York attend his funeral more than twenty years following the verdict.

The two key areas on which the case was based firstly involved the attitude of the Rebbe towards acquiring wealth. Here Rabbi Jacobs, in his testimony, contrasts Chabad with other Hasidic sects suggesting that this was met with disdain and that therefore the notion of a personal transfer of wealth from one generation to another was completely anathema. The second central piece of evidence concerned the composition of the library itself. Given that the sort of books and manuscripts contained within the collection included literature covering Communist propaganda and secular history for example it was strongly advanced by Rabbi Jacobs that the library was gathered not for personal gain but for use by the community. Here too we see the demonstration of an openness to matters far outside of their immediate concern.

Rabbi Dr Jacobs' important part of this case is now here for all to see along with his wonderful explanations as to the Chabad movement's origins and historical development.

Simon Eder, our Director, and myself have run sessions where we talk through the main points of the case. Simon being the examiner and me being my father!

Ivor Jacobs
Trustee, Friends of LouisJacobs.org
London, England

```
                                                          468

 1   UNITED STATES DISTRICT COURT
     EASTERN DISTRICT OF NEW YORK
 2   - - - - - - - - - - - - - - - - X
 3   AGUDAS CHASIDEI CHABAD
     OF UNITED STATES,                    :
 4
                   Plaintiff,             :
 5
              -against-                   :    CV 85 2909
 6
     BARRY S. GOURARY,                    :
 7
                   Defendant,             :
 8
     HANNA GOURARY,                       :
 9
                   Intervenor-            :
10                 Defendant
11   - - - - - - - - - - - - - - - - X
12                        United States Courthouse
                          Brooklyn, New York
13
                          December 5th, 1985
14                        9:30 o'clock a.m.
15
16   B E F O R E:
17          HONORABLE CHARLES P. SIFTON, U.S.D.J.
18
19
20
21
22
23
24                      GENE RUDOLPH
                   Official Court Reporter
25
```

APPEARANCES:

 MILLER, CASSIDY, LARROCA & LEWIN
 Attorneys for Plaintiff
 2555 M. Street, N.W., Suite 500
 Washington, D.C. 20037

 BY: NATHAN LEWIN, ESQ.
   SETH P. WAXMAN, ESQ.
   of Counsel

 SCHNADER, HARRISON, SEGAL & LEWIS
 Attorneys for Plaintiff
 1600 Market Street
 Suite 3600
 Philadelphia, Pennsylvania 19103

 BY: JEROME J. SHESTACK, ESQ.
   of Counsel

 STROOCK & STROOCK & LAVAN
 Attorneys for Defendant
 and Intervenor-Defendant
 7 Hanover Square
 New York, New York 10004

 BY: ALVIN HELLERSTEIN, ESQ.
   BRIAN M. COGAN, ESQ.
   ELIZABETH A. MULLINS, ESQ.
   of Counsel

      oOo

470

1 THE COURT: All right. Do you want to
2 call the witness who was going to be taken out of
3 order?
4 MR. LEWIN: Yes. Rabbi Jacobs.
5 Before we do that Your Honor, we did
6 hand up to the Court yesterday at the close of the
7 session our English translation of exhibit -- let's
8 see if I can find it. Exhibit 438 and 439 and if
9 Your Honor could read that, the witness will be
10 referring to that exhibit at some point during his
11 expert testimony. So that happened at the very end
12 of the session. I don't know whether Your Honor has
13 had a chance to read that.
14 THE COURT: I did read that last night.
15 MR. LEWIN: All right.
16 With that, we'd be calling Dr. Louis
17 Jacobs.
18 THE COURT: All right.
19 Would you come up, sir, and be sworn or
20 have the oath administered to you.

Jacobs-direct-Shestack

L O U I S   J A C O B S,
called as a witness, having been first duly affirmed, was examined and testified as follows:

DIRECT EXAMINATION
BY MR. SHESTACK:

Q   Dr. Jacobs, what is your current position?
A   I am the Rabbi of a synagogue in London, New London Synagogue, London, England and Professor of Talmud at Leo Baeck College for the training of rabbis in London.
Q   And what are you doing in the United States at this time?
A   I am visiting professor at the Harvard Divinity School.
Q   What are you teaching at the Harvard Divinity School?
A   I am teaching courses in Jewish law, the principles of Jewish faith, Jewish mysticism and Talmudic reasoning.
Q   Thank you.
    I'd like to go through your qualifications, Dr. Jacobs, and with his Honor's permission, if there is no objection, I may do a little leading in order to move it quickly through the qualifications.

Jacobs-direct-Shestack

THE COURT: All right.
Q   Where were you born?
A   Manchester, England.
Q   Would you tell the Court what your early education and then higher education was?
A   I was educated at Manchester Central High School, at London University, and at Manchester Talmudical College.
Q   Do you have a rabbinical diploma?
A   Yes.
Q   Where is that from?
A   From the Manchester Talmudical College and from the head of the rabbinic course of Manchester.
Q   You have a BA and PHD and would you tell us where they are from?
A   The BA is from London University, in Semitics, and PHD from London University.
Q   Could you tell us, briefly, some of the universities that you have lectured at?
A   I have lectured at Oxford and Cambridge in England, and Harvard, of course, here, and Chicago, Albany, various other universities in the United States.
Q   You also have a -- some connection with Hebrew University in Jerusalem?

Jacobs-direct-Shestack

A My friends endowed a scholarship in Jewish mysticism in my name at the Hebrew University.

Q Would you tell us some of the honorary offices and learned societies that you belong to?

A I was former president of the British Association of Jewish Studies. And former president of the London Society for the Study of Religion.

Q And do you occupy any present position on any learned society?

A I'm a member of the Council of the -- of the London Society for study of religion.

Q The Society for Jewish Study?

A I'm the vice-president of the Society for Jewish Study.

Q Have you won any prizes for your works in --

A Yes. I won the Hillel Zeitlan prize for the best book on religion, and the Jewish Chronicle Award for the best book of the year.

Q Are you doing any editing, Dr. Jacobs?

A I'm one of the editors of the Littman Library for the Jewish Civilization.

Q What is the Littman library of Jewish --

A The Littman library is a -- an endowment by a prominent lawyer in England to publish books of scholarly interest on Jewish topics.

Jacobs-direct-Shestack

Q And are you also -- turning to some of your books, what are the areas in which you have written?

A I have written mainly in three areas. First, books on Jewish theology. One of them is called Jewish Theology. The other is called the Principles of the Jewish Faith.

I have written on Talmudic reasoning, book called Talmudic Argument and book called Studies in Talmudic Logic and Methodology, and the third area is in Jewish mysticism, which embraces the Kabbala and Chasidism.

Q Would you tell us some of your works in this third area, dealing with Chasidism and mysticism?

A I have translated with an introduction and notes a Chasidic classic, Actually a Chabad classic called Tract on Ecstasy. That was the English title. It's a study by the second Rebbe of the movement, Chabad. It's a profound investigation into different types of ecstasy during prayer and contemplation, and I have also done a study which I call Seeker of Unity, of the most distinguished pupil of the first Rebbe, the founder of Chabad movement called Starroselje.

Q Some others?

A And I have -- I have translated with an

Jacobs-direct-Shestack

introduction -- lengthy intro and notes, some Jewish Mystical Testimonies, the book is called Jewish Mystical Testimonies, and the point is that Jewish -- the Jewish mystics were very reticent about their own experiences and there are only a very few actual bearings of the soul, as it were, and I have translated these, similar to things like the writings of St. Teresa or St. John of the Cross.

Q   Have you written on Chasidic prayer?

A   I have written on -- I wrote a book called Chasidic Prayer.

Q   Does that also deal with prayer in the Chabad movement?

A   It deals with prayer in the Chasidic movement generally and there is a chapter on prayer in Chabad.

Q   Have you contributed to encyclopedias?

A   Yes, I have contributed to -- especially to the Encyclopedia Judaica, to which I have contributed many articles.

Q   Dr. Jacobs, there is attached to a trial brief that the plaintiff filed in this case and which therefore is in the record an article from the 1975-1976 Encyclopedia Judaica Yearbook.

I show you that article and ask you

Jacobs-direct-Shestack

1 whether you were the author of that article?
2 A   Yes, I am the author of that article.
3   MR. SHESTACK: If Your Honor will note,
4 that's attached the our trial brief as an appendix.
5 appendix.
6   THE COURT: I'm sure I've got a copy.
7   All right. Go ahead. Yes, I see it.
8 Q   Have you also contributed to any other
9 encyclopedias?
10 A   I have contributed a number of articles to a new
11 encyclopedia that's being published by McMillian,
12 called the Encyclopedia of Religions, edited by
13 Marcia Eliade.
14 Q   Without going into great detail, could you
15 briefly mention some of the learned journals for whom
16 you have written?
17 A   Journal of Jewish Studies, Journal of Semitic
18 Studies, Judaism, Conservative Judaism, and others.
19   MR. SHESTACK: Your Honor, we submit
20 Dr. Jacobs as an expert.
21   Is there any voir dire on his
22 qualifications?
23   MR. HELLERSTEIN: No.
24   THE COURT: I beg your pardon?
25   MR. HELLERSTEIN: No.

                                                              477
                        Jacobs-direct-Shestack
1   THE COURT: No questions.
2   All right. Go ahead.
3   MR. SHESTACK: Thank you, Your Honor.
4   Q   Dr. Jacobs, are you familiar with Chabad
5   literature?
6   A   Yes.
7   Q   By the way, when we use the words "Chabad
8   Chasidism," is that the same as Lubavitch Chasidism?
9   A   Yes.
10   The point here is that Chabad was the
11   name given to the movement during the time of its
12   founder, Rabbi Schneur Zalman of Liadi. The second
13   Rebbe, his son, who was known as the middle Rebbe,
14   settled in the town of Lubavitch and his successors
15   lived in Lubavitch. Hence, Lubavitch is the name of
16   the town. It was quite usual in Chasidism to call
17   the movement after the town in which the Rebbes
18   resided.
19   Q   So it is correct to say that sometimes you use
20   the word Lubavitch Chasidism, sometimes Chabad
21   Chasidism?
22   A   They are synonymous.
23   Q   By way of background --
24   A   Well, can I just answer that?
25   They are synonymous today and have been

Jacobs-direct-Shestack

for sometime. It is also true that there were Chabad masters who were descendants of the Rebbe who did not live in Lubavitch and in fact founded separate dynasties so from that point of view Chabad is more general than Lubavitch.

Q By way of background, we have used the word in this proceeding "Torah" and sometimes "Mishna," other sources of Jewish law.

Could you briefly explain to the Court what Torah encompasses and also what are the main sources of Jewish law and learning today?

A The word "Torah" means teaching and in its original meaning, it's referred to the Pentateuch, the five books of Moses. Later it referred the whole of the Hebrew bible, the old testament, and then the doctrine was eventually developed that there is an oral Torah. That is to say, there is a traditional interpretation of the written text, which is also part of the Torah, and this is found deposited chiefly in the two works known as the Mishna and the Talmud.

Q Would you tell us what the Mishna is first?

A The Mishna is a kind of digest of Judaism compiled at the end of the second century. The Talmud, commentary on the Mishna of which there are

two parts or two Talmuds. One is the Palestinian
compiled around about the year four hundred. The
other, Babylonian compounded about the year five
hundred and they are said to be from additionally the
summary of the oral Torah so that the Torah then
consists of the written text of the bible and its
interpretation as found in the Talmudic literature,
and eventually the word "Torah" became synonymous
with Judaism.

In other words, any sacred literature or
thoughts or ideas or doctrines that are accepted by
the community of believers become part of the Torah.

Q   And would you elaborate just a little bit on
what the Talmud is?

A   The Talmud is the summary of all the
discussions, chiefly of a legal nature, but not
entirely so, of the rabbis in Palestine, the
first -- from the third to the fourth -- third and
fourth centuries and in Babylon, from the third to
the fifth, end of the fifth century.

Q   Has the -- all the law in the Talmud been
codified?

A   Codified is not quite the right word. The
Talmud is not a code of law. It is a record of
decisions and discussions chiefly. It's

Jacobs-direct-Shestack

1 theoretical.
2 　　　　　　The -- what one should say is that the
3 teachings of the Talmud have been codified in various
4 codes of law. Like that of Maimonides in the 12th
5 century and more particularly in the work known as
6 the Shulchan Aruch, the arranged table, which was
7 compiled in the 16th century. That became the
8 standard code of Jewish law.
9 Q   And is the Shulchan Aruch the primary source of
10 Jewish law at this stage?
11 A   Yes.
12 Q   You're familiar with Chabad literature, is that
13 correct?
14 A   Yes.
15 Q   Are you a Lubavitcher yourself?
16 A   No.
17 Q   You've had Chabad teachers?
18 A   I had two Chabad teachers.
19 Q   Could you tell the Court what the principal --
20 some of the principal works in Chabad literature
21 are?
22 A   Well, the standard work, the classical work of
23 Chabad is the Tanya by the founder of the movement.
24 This is studied and has been commented on by
25 followers of the movement ever since it was

published.

Then there are the other works of the founder, Schneur Zalman. They are in the nature of commentaries chiefly on the Torah.

Then there are the many works of the second Rebbe, who was known as the middle Rebbe, and then there are the works of the Tzemach Tzedek who is the third Rebbe of the movement, who wrote in addition to his -- his Chasidic doctrines and teachings, responsa, that is, legal decisions, and all this has been published, and each Rebbe in fact has contributed to the great mass of material that is Chabad literature.

Q   There are thousands of such writings which are the writings of Rebbes?

A   I don't know about thousands. But certainly voluminous literature.

Q   How does the Chabad literature in volume compare with literature of other Chasidic groups?

A   Immensely greater than any other group.

Q   In your view --

A   The point is, I think, in this connection, that most of the Chasidic writing we have from other groups is really records of their -- of their sermons which they gave on Sabbath afternoons and they were -- they

Jacobs-direct-Shestack

could not be written down on the Sabbath, afternoon. They were written down afterwards and published. So each Rebbe, each famous Rebbe has a number of works to his credit, which are attributed to him in the sense that he is the originator of them although not necessarily the author.

In Chabad it was quite different. The Rebbes from the time of the founder actually wrote works of exposition of Chabad doctrine. The Rebbe Schneur Zalman the founder did preicsely that. The Tanya is unlike any other Chasidic work at the time in that it is a more or less systematic presentation of Chasidic thought.

Q   Is the Tanya used by Chabad today?

A   Oh, yes. Yes. I mean, no Chabad Chasid would be out without a copy of his Tanya. It's been translated into a number of languages.

Q   In order to understand the Chabad movement and its philosophy, would you regard it as important, unimportant, critical, not critical, to be familiar with Chabad literature?

A   Unimportant -- I don't follow.

Q   What is the significance -- what is the necessity of being versed in Chabad literature in order to expound on its philosophy?

Jacobs-direct-Shestack

A   Oh, sure. Since it's a very intricate and complicated system, I would say, to understand it correctly, it requires years of study.

Also, we must not forget that the language is a kind of mixture of Hebrew and Aramaic, Rabbinic, Rabbinic Hebrew, Aramaic, together with many Kabbalistic terms that would be quite undecipherable to those who are not initiated into the movement.

So it more than -- certainly more than -- I would say, that this applies to any Chasidic Torah, but it applies specifically to Chabad teaching because of the profundity of the subject and because of the difficulty in mastering it.

Q   Dr. Jacobsa, apart from yourself and apart from people who are in the Chabad movement itself, do you know of many scholars who are not members of Chabad who have written about Chabad or Chabad literature?

A   Yes. There are a number of women who have written on Chabad at the Hebrew University. There is a young woman who is, I would say, quite an authority on Chabad called Rachel Leior but then the point here is that at the Hebrew University, Jewish Mysticism, that includes Chasidism studied as an academic subject. I

Jacobs-direct-Shestack

would say that's the way of studying it for a long
time.
Q   Are you familiar with the name Dr. Arthur
Green?
A   Yes.
Q   Has he, to your knowledge, written on Chabad
literature?
A   Not -- certainly not extensively. He's an
authority on Nachman of Bratslav, written a fine work of
Nachman of Bratslav called the Tormented Master and has
written on the -- Rebbe Nachman of Chernobyl.
Q   I will ask you at a later stage to compare
Nachman of Bratslav with the Chabad movement, so let's
hold that.
        Are you familiar with a professor by the
name of Menachem Friedman?
A   No.
Q   As far as now, has he written anything in
Chasidism?
A   Not to my knowledge.
Q   Now, in connection with this case, did you have
opportunity to review various of the documents in
what have been identified here as the white volume,
the blue volume and the red volume?
A   I have seen all three volumes. I have read

Jacobs-direct-Shestack

them through virtually from cover to cover.
Q   In connection with your testimony here, did you have occasion to meet with Mr. Lewin and myself?
A   Yes.
Q   And with Dr. Levine?
A   Yes.
Q   Anybody else?
A   Various people in the -- belonging to the Chabad movement.
Q   You've had an opportunity also to look at the library that's in issue here?
A   Yes, I have.
Q   Are you being compensated in connection with the work you have done to prepare your testimony and to testify here today?
A   Yes.
Q   And with whom did you work out that compensation?
A   With you and Mr. Levine.
Q   Mr. Lewin?
A   Mr. Lewin.
Q   Thank you.
         Now, turning more directly to the matters here and although still as a background, before we get to the Chabad, could you define for the

The Original 1985 Courtroom Testimony

Jacobs-direct-Shestack

Court briefly what is Chasidism? I'll ask you to
make your answers brief because I don't want to
infringe on what another expert witness might testify
to but generally what is Chasidism?

A   It's difficult to answer that, but one would
have to say that it was a revivalist movement in
Judaism which arose in the 18th century. The word
"Chasid" originally meant a superior type of person
to a Tzaddik, Tzaddik simply being a good man, the
Chasid someone who is extraordinarily good, one
might say a saint. But for various reasons we need
not go into now, the founder of the movement, Israel
Baal Shem Tov, the founder of the movement, Israel
Baal Shem Tov became known as the Tzaddik so the word
"Tzaddik" became the name for the saint, and
consequently the roles are reversed.

The Chasid then became a follower. A
follower of a particular master whom the Chasid
believed would lead him nearer to God. And the --
essentially Chasidic doctrine is that the power of
God, the vitality of the Almighty pervades the whole
universe and that the aim of human beings is to -- to
be with God in the mind at all times insofar as this
is possible, since this is extremely difficult. The
idea developed that it -- the ordinary Chasid could

Jacobs-direct-Shestack

1 be assisted in this by being associated with a
2 Tzadik who in turn was associated with the Almighty.
3 Q   Now, you mentioned the aim being to relate to
4 the deity?
5 A   Yes.
6 Q   What is the term the "D'veykut?"
7 A   The D'veykut is the term that is used in this
8 context and it means, comes from a root "davak," DA
9 VA K, meaning to be attached. So that davak means
10 being attached to God, attached to God in the sense
11 that God is in the mind at all times.
12 Q   Now, you also said that the founder was the Baal
13 Shem Tov. Is there an acronym by which the Baal Shem Tov
14 is often referred?
15 A   He is often referred to as the Besht. But
16 actually this is only, as far as I know in English
17 writings. I don't know that Chasidim ever refer to
18 him as the Besht. It is an acronym for Baal Shem Tov.
19 Q   About when did Baal Shem Tov live?
20 A   He died in 1760.
21 Q   And what happened after that? Could you tell
22 us about his successor?
23 A   Yes. After his death, we have a number of
24 disciples, any one of whom could have been the new
25 leader of the movement. In fact, the great organizer

Jacobs-direct-Shestack

of the movement and in a sense therefore, the real founder was the man known as Dov Baer of Mezeritch. He's known as the Maggid, Maggid meaning a preacher. He had great organizing talents, gathered around him a number of very distinguished Chasidim who in their turn became Rebbes. That is, leaders of the movement in the sense that they spread throughout Eastern Europe and each one set up a court as it is called in his vicinity, each with Chasidim.

Q Now, what happened after the death of the Maggid?

A That's -- after the death of the Maggid, these disciples set up a court of their own.

Q Were there different groups of the Chasidic movement formed?

A Oh, yes. There was -- since each was -- each one of these disciples had his own particular way, as they call it, his own way of looking at Judaism and at Chasidism, you have a rich variety, so much so that in a way, one can only talk about the Chasidic movement in a very loose sense.

It's rather like Judaism. Many different branches of Judaism, many different branches of Chasidism, depending on the temperament, ideas, doctrines stressed by each particular Rebbe.

Jacobs-direct-Shestack

Q   Could you draw an analogy to Protestantism in that regard?

A   Yes. I think the analogy is not unhelpful.

Q   So it would be --

A   Where you have --

Q   Very specific groups?

A   The difference would only be that there, it -- less would depend on the personalities. I mean, Methodists are not Wesleyans in that sense. Whereas, in Chasidism, the differences resulted from the differences of approach to the theory by the different Rebbes.

Q   You're referring to John Wessley, the founder of Methodism?

A   Yes.

Q   Now, how was, when the -- Chasidism that then started in the 18th century and how was it regarded by the remainder of the Jewish world at the time this movement arose?

A   The traditional rabbis were known as the Mitnagdim.

Q   What does Mitnagdim mean?

A   It means opponents.

Q   Opponents of Chasidism?

A   They were opponents of Chasidism and their

Jacobs-direct-Shestack

opposition was on various grounds.

Q   Who gave them that name, do you know?

A   The --

Q   The Chasidim?

A   We don't really know that. We do know that at quite an early period, they were called Mitnagdim. In a way, I --

Q   I guess I -- I had the impression by analogy that Protestants were Protestants and that name was given to them by Catholics?

A   The analogy is very interesting. Of course they were, the Protestants were protesting against what was sort of the establishment. Here, the -- some scholars have seen this as the -- great victory of Chasidism that instead of them being called the Mitnagdim, the opponents, the Protestants, it was their opponents who were the -- the establishment who were called the Mitnagdim but I don't know about that.

Q   Go on to how they were regarded?

A   They were regarded as -- in the early period, they were regarded as heretics. Chiefly, chiefly on the grounds of their theological doctrine, which is called by some scholars, and I have used the term Pantheism. Calm is in God. In the Chasidic view the whole universe exists in God. This is different from Pantheism, in that in Pantheism, God is just a name one gives to the totality of things so God and the universe are identical. In Chasidism, God is the all and the universe is -- exists in God, as it were, so that in a way, there is no ultimate reality except God and the aim of the Chasid is to pierce the veils of appearances and get nearer to the reality that is God.

Now, the opponents of the movement felt that this was contrary to Jewish teaching in that if you say God is everywhere and He's in all things, it would follow that He is in -- unclean things and in fact, you find again and again that the Mitnagdim say that this doctrine will lead to people thinking of the Torah in unclean places, and what they meant by that was that if you stress the idea that God is all, you tend to obliterate the distinction between good and evil, or the demarcation lines between good and evil and that was chiefly the proposition.

There were also social grounds because the Chasidim tended to form groups of their own and break away from what was called the K'lal, which was the establishment, leaders of the community, so there was a social side to it as well.

Jacobs-direct-Shestack

But chiefly I would say it was theological.

Q Then, going back, coming then to the 19th century and the early 20th, how did it all work out?

A How did it all work out? Well, Chasidism had a tremendous appeal.

Q That's perhaps not a very scientific question. But --

A Well --

Q A shortcut?

A I think I know what you mean. Chasidism had tremendous appeal to the ordinary devout Jew because unlike the traditional Jewish view that you couldn't get anywhere, as it were, unless you were a great Talmudic scholar, Chasidism said that God is near to every Jew who is -- who approaches him in sincerity and in truth and consequently, this brought religion very close and even I would say mysticism very close to the masses of Jews. The result being that by the turn of the last century, about the year 1800, Chasidism had succeeded in conquering about half of the communities of Eastern Europe.

Q Could you bring us up-to-date, tell us generally what you regard the status of the Chasidic

Jacobs-direct-Shestack

1 movement today in Judaism?
2 A   There are groups of Chasidim all over the
3 world. I am not familiar with -- I can't quote
4 numbers. But there is a -- there seems to be a great
5 popularity.
6 Q   And it is a strong -- would you regard it as a
7 strong and legitimate expression of Judaism today?
8 A   That's not for me to say really. But I mean,
9 what does one mean by "legitimate expression" of
10 Judaism? There are many varieties of expression and
11 insofar as it exists, I would say it is a legitimate
12 expression of Judaism. If you mean is there value in
13 it, sure there is value in it.
14 Q   We will come to the value in a moment.
15   Now, I don't want you to take very much
16 time on this next question because another witness,
17 Mr. Wiesel, will be testifying on it.
18   But can you briefly identify some of the
19 branches of Chasidism? Then we will come to Chabad.
20 A   Other branches than --
21 Q   Than Chabad?
22 A   Than Chabad. There are have many. But to -- I
23 suppose I should just mention those that are fairly
24 popular today.
25   There is Ger. There is Belz, B E L Z,

Jacobs-direct-Shestack

there is Sotmar, there is Vishnitz, and there is -- I think there is quite a -- a group of Chasidim known as Sadegora. There are many -- Bobov, there is Bobov.

Q   All right.
        Let's now --
A   And many others, smaller groups.
Q   Now let's turn to Chabad, with that background, and would you give the Court the early history of the Chabad movement?
A   Well, I would say that Chabad is in some sense is a new movement, although it's -- it's always considered itself to be part of Chasidism. It is part of the Chasidic movement but in some ways, it's a departure, departure in this sense, that the ideas are certainly those presumably of the founder. We don't know too much about the original ideas of the founder, but certainly Rabbi Schneur Zalman, the founder of the movement, did not claim that he was inventing a new movement. He was building.
Q   Let me stop just for a moment.
        Would you identify, although I think he's been identified, Schneur Zalman, approximately what period he was -- he was the first Rebbe of Chabad?

Jacobs-direct-Shestack

1 A   He was the first Rebbe of Chabad. He was the
2 disciple of the Maggid of Mezeritz we mentioned
3 before. And he -- he died in 19 -- in 1813.
4 Q   How is he often referred to in the Chabad
5 movement?
6 A   As the Alter Rebbe, the old Rebbe.
7 Q   Alter is the --
8 A   Alter is old. The old Rebbe. The founder of
9 the movement, so he was -- he didn't claim to be
10 entirely original, but he was original in this sense,
11 that he was systematic expounder of the ideas of the
12 movement unlike the others.
13   So he -- he developed in a systematic
14 way this doctrine that I mentioned before of
15 Pantheism and it's nowhere expressed more forcibly
16 than in his writings and the writings of his
17 disciples and descendants.
18 Q   Dr. Jacobs, we have used the word "Rabbi"
19 sometimes and then the word "Rebbe."
20   Would you just explain to the Court how
21 "Rabbi" is used and how "Rebbe" is used?
22 A   Rabbi is the name given to traditional rabbi
23 whose function is to give decisions in Jewish law.
24   It was certainly not unusual in the past
25 for people to refer to the rabbi in Hebrew Harav, to

Jacobs-direct-Shestack

refer to him as Rebbe which simply meant, "my teacher."

But with the rise of Chasidism you had a new type of leader. His function was no longer to decide Jewish law unless he was a rabbi and some of them were rabbis. But his function was a new one, although Chasidim would say that it's old. But from the historical point of view it was a new idea, that you have a kind of -- oh, it has been compared to a guru, sort of saintly guide, to this spiritual life and he could no longer -- he was called the Tzaddik as we have seen, but another name for him was the name Rebbe, to distinguish him from the Rabbi, from the Rav, the traditional Rabbi. The traditional rabbi and this term is found in the earliest documents, so it's not something of later development.

Q At each particular time, there was only one Rebbe, while the movement may have many rabbis, is that correct?

A That's right, yes.

In each Chasidic group you only have one Rebbe and he is the supreme authority. Many of his followers will be rabbis. And he himself may be a rabbi but that's incidental.

Q And the followers, Chasidim are the followers

Jacobs-direct-Shestack

1 of a particular Rebbe?
2 A   Yes. You can't -- you can't be a Chasid
3 without having a Rebbe because as we have seen, the
4 term "Chasid" came to mean a follower, follower of a
5 Rebbe. So although, for example, Martin Buber and
6 others have tried to work out a neochasidic
7 philosophy without commenting on its value or
8 otherwise, it's not Chasidism because there is no
9 such thing as a Chasid without a Rebbe.
10 Q   Now, what is the -- I think you have mentioned
11 in connection with Schneur Zalman that he developed
12 an intellectual movement.
13   Could you amplify on that and in terms
14 of the unique aspects of Chabad?
15 A   Basically I would say this, that from my
16 reading of Chabad literature, the word "Chabad"
17 means -- is an acronym for Chochma, Bina, Daas.
18 Q   Which means?
19 A   Which means wisdom, understanding and
20 knowledge, used in a technical sense that we need not
21 go into here. The chief point is that in the
22 Kabbala, that's the mystical system, you have the
23 idea that in the divine process, that there is first
24 a divine thought, the processes of divine thought
25 which is Chabad, wisdom, understanding and

Jacobs-direct-Shestack

knowledge. Then there are the -- those processes which on the analogy with the human are called emotional and in Chasidic thought to some extent in earlier Jewish not in the Kabbala, all the divine processes are mirrored in the soul of man, in the soul of human beings, and consequently, there are two ways of approaching God, two ways of approaching religion.

One is through emotion, through experience, and the other is through contemplation.

Now, Chabad is chiefly a contemplative movement. That is to say, the Chasid is expected to dwell long in his prayers in contemplation of the whole divine scheme as seen in the Kabbala and in the belief of Chabad that the religious feelings will be stirred not so much in themselves but will be stirred by this profound contemplation.

The Chabad leaders stressed that you do not approach it the other way round. You don't try to whip up enthusiasm and then hope that you'll understand. But you have to contemplate and understand and then any religious emotion that results from it will be authentic. Otherwise, it will be shallow. It will be unauthentic.

Q   Is there a special intellectual emphasis in

Jacobs-direct-Shestack

Chabad that is not present in other Chasidic movements?

A   Yes. This is the very point. This is -- this was one of the issues between Chasidism and most other groups, between Chabad and most other groups of Chasidism because most of the other groups did claim that the Baal Shem Tov, the founder of the Chasidic movement was teaching that the emotions were extremely valuable and in fact, they criticized Chabad for dwelling too much on matters on high instead of being concerned with the practical, practicalities in the emotional sense of religious life.

But Chabad has always prided itself on having this different approach.

I would say, because of their different approach it is virtually a different movement.

Q   Now, how would this emphasis on the divine every moment and the intellectual aspect manifest itself in Chabad life?

A   It manifests itself, it seems to me, in a particular doctrine, which is found to some extent in other Chasidic traditions, but which is particularly emphasized in Chabad. This is the doctrine that is known as annihilation of self, which means the

Jacobs-direct-Shestack

transcendence of the grasping ego of man in order to meet with the divine and in the Chabad thought particularly you get the idea that deep in the recesses of the human soul there is a portion, a portion of God.

The divine spark in man is taken in a rather literal fashion, that -- so that when the -- when the ego is transcended what happens is the divine in the soul{g} meets the divine in the universe.

Q   Now, you had mentioned the founder of g Chabad, the first Rebbe, and who was his successor?

A   His successor was the Rebbe known as the middle Rebbe, his son, Dov Ber.

Q   Where did he --

A   He settled in Lubavitch.

Q   And I think you earlier mentioned that settling in Lubavitch was the reason why the movement took on the Lubavitch name?

A   Yes, yes.

Q   And succeeding Rebbes at least until the modern era, they lived in Lubavitch?

A   Yes. Yes. In any event, Chasidic groups were called, where the -- where the first Rebbes resided, like Ger and Bobov.

Jacobs-direct-Shestack

Q   Can you -- the high state that Chabad adheres
aspires to, who reaches that state? How does that
manifest itself?

A   I think that the Chabad followers would say
that it's impossible to reach that stage without the
help of a Rebbe and I think many of them would say
some of the Rebbes could reach that stage but the
Chasid is helped to reach that stage by being
associated with the Rebbe so you get a kind of
hierarchy. The Chasid is close to the Rebbe. The
Rebbe is close to God and therefore, the Chasid is
closer to God than he would be if he were not a
Chasid.

Q   The Rebbe acts as the guide, exemplar for
the --

A   The Rebbe acts as a guide. But -- but guide is
not the sole function. The Rebbe also prays on
behalf of his followers and there is the belief that
his prayers are particularly effective.

(Continued on next page.)

502

Jacobs-direct/Shestack

1 Q In terms of a transcendentalist philosophy,
2 how would you explain that, transcending the ego
3 and worshipping God. Can it be explained in those
4 terms?
5 A Yes.
6 The idea is that man is imprisoned
7 within his ego. This is not only peculiar to
8 Jewish mystiscism. All mystics are saying things
9 like this. The way to reach the divine is to
10 escape the prison cell, the prison cell of the
11 ego. And that's what annhilation of the self is.
12 It means reaching the deeper self.
13 Q You mentioned the tract of ecstasy. What is
14 that role in Chabad philosophy? What is the Hebrew
15 word for ecstasy?
16 A I translated the word used hispallilot as
17 ecstasy, which I think is a fair translation.
18 Others may translate it differently.
19 But in any event, what the Rebbe was
20 saying in this remarkable document --
21 Q Who wrote it?
22 A The Mittler Rebbe. And he is advising his
23 followers how to distinguish between authentic
24 ecstasy and sham ecstasy.
25 He is aware that there are religious

Jacobs-direct/Shestack

people including many of his followers who believed they obtained some religious experience and even shouted it in their prayers and exaltation and really were fooling themselves.

What he says is if you are aware of it you have not had the experience. You only had the experience if you have sufficiently transcending the ego. But he believed that ecstasy was important. And it had to come -- that's where Chabad comes it. It had to come from the contemporary life rather than the emotions.

Q   Which is a unique aspect of Chabad?

A   Yes.

Q   Could you comment on the role of education in Chabad Judaism?

A   Meditation?

Q   Education.

A   Education.

Since it's the intellectual movement in Chasidism, it follows that education is important. Education is important for all Chasidic groups and all orthodox Jews, the study of the Torah is of extreme religious value. But in Chabad it is not alone the study of the traditional sources, Bible, Talmud, Code and so forth, but involves the

Jacobs-direct/Shestack

1 Chasidic functions as well, which in this instance
2 means the Chabad doctrines.
3 Q   What to your knowledge has Chabad adherence
4 done to promote education to the extent that --
5 A   It is enormous.
6   There is the publishing house, books
7 have been published in many languages. The
8 reprints of classical works of the movement. There
9 is an educational network in practically every
10 large city or even small cities all over the
11 world.
12   So, that even those of us who don't
13 necessarily agree with every detail of Chabad
14 philosophy would still feel that it is worthy of
15 admiration.
16 Q   What about the establishment of yeshivot and
17 explain what a yeshiva is?
18 A   A yeshiva is a place where students -- where
19 there are higher studies of the Torah, and that is
20 the Torah for more mature students.
21   And there are yeshivot in many parts of
22 the world, and in Europe in the pre-war days. It
23 is a place which is somewhat translated as a
24 college. It is somewhat like a college. It is a
25 place where young men would study the Torah for

Jacobs-direct/Shestack

years on end.

The Lubavitch movement has yeshivot of a particular kind. In so far as the main subject, whose study is the Talmud they resemble all other yeshivot.

But insofar as there is a special emphasis on the Chasidic way and especially the Chabad way and on the Chabad doctrine, they are in that way different from other yeshivot.

Q During the period before the headquarters of the Chabad movement came to the United States and during the Russian period of the 1920's when the Soviet government had already been established, what happened to the Chabad efforts for education during that period?

MR. HELLERSTEIN: If you please, I object to the form of the question. I don't know what period of time we are dealing with.

MR. SHESTACK: I am dealing with the period of the Russian Revolution which came about around 1917, and the Union of Soviet Socialist Republics has been prevailing a form of government since that time.

THE COURT: It sounds like testimony more than a question.

Jacobs-direct/Shestack

Let's just confine this to the period of the 1920's, if that's appropriate.

Q   Would you please do so, Doctor Jacobs.

A   Yes.

It is fairly well known that the Chabad people in Russia, Soviet Russia, virtually risked their lives in order to propagate Judaism and Chasidism. And I don't know how they did it; but they somehow managed to preserve many of these traditions of Judaism, including yeshivot of a sort.

Q   Now, in Chabad, what are the roles of organization in Chabad life, the communal organization? Would you please explain that, about elaborate on that?

A   We don't know the type of organization that was there in the very early periods, although from various references in the writings of the founder and the son, it is clear there was an organization in the sense that somebody saw to it that the teachings were written down or copied, disseminated and printed, and the courts of the Rebbe were kept up.

As the years progressed there was greater organization. And I think to my knowledge

Jacobs-direct/Shestack

the greatest organizer of the movement was the previous Rebbe.

Q   Rabbi Joseph Isaac Schneersohn?

A   Joseph Isaac Schneersohn.

Q   And would you tell us why you said that?

A   It was due to his inspiration and efforts that the movement spread and the movement was well established.

I can only speak from my knowledge from the newspapers and accounts of that kind, and from what basically everybody knows, and from my teachers that you mentioned who lived in England, in Manchester, but who were obviously parts of an organization in the sense that they corresponded with the Rebbe and had had complete confidence in the Rebbe and saw themselves as part of a fraternity and this could not be done without organization.

Q   Now, let's turn to a subject that has figured in this proceedings called maamad.

Generally could you tell us how that term is used by the Lubavitch community?

A   The "maamad" comes from the root, maamad, to stand, and therefore could mean to support, to keep standing.

Jacobs-direct/Shestack

And it is used for the -- the plural is maamadoth or maamados as is said in Chabad parlance. It is a due, D U E, for which every member of the movement is expected to consider himself responsible, and he has to pay so much -- as far as I know it is not a fixed sum, but there is an amount according to means which every member pays or is expected to pay. And this contributes -- people were sent out to collect the sums. And the money was for the support of the Rebbe's court.

Q Going back a little bit, what is the basis for the term maamad? Is it found in biblical usage?

A This is not clear to me, nor is it, I don't think, to anyone else, why the term maamad was used for this.

However, there are two instances of the use of this term in the earlier period, of which those who used it must have been aware --

Q Earlier periods meaning what?

A The earlier period, the Talmudic period.

Q All right.

A One is according to the Talmud when a sacrifice was offered in the temple on behalf of the community there had to be priests and levites, the priests that offer the sacrafice, the levites to play the musical instruments, and there had to be representatives of the people. And these were called "Anshei ha'maamad," the people of the maamad.

So, in that sense there I think the meaning is that they stood beside the sacrifice and they stood in on behalf of the people. That's one usage.

The other one, which is perhaps more relevant is the passage in the Talmud which says that if communal property, like a synagogue, is being sold, it can only be sold by the seven good men of the city; the mayor and the council.

Q That's all they could find in the city?

A They limited to ten -- to seven. They limited it to seven, seven being a mystical number presumably. But it had to be done in the presence of the men in the city. And the Hebrew is "ba'maamad", in the presence.

That doesn't necessarily mean they had to consult every member of the community, but it had to be done with their consent. The meaning is that the seven good men in the city could not

Jacobs-direct/Shestack

merely dispose of communal property like a synagogue without consulting the citizens as a whole.

It seems to me that these terms are so well known that it is extremely unlikely, although I cannot state it categorically, that it is extremely likely when they use maamad I do think they at least by association had that in mind.

Q   It is not exactly clear to me.

You needed the consent of seven good men to sell a synagogue, and why would you --

A   That's the point.

Since it was communal property and everybody had a share in it, it wouldn't do simply for the delegate of authorities to dispose of it. It had to be done with the kind of votes of the whole community.

Q   Now, we have seen the term "maamad" in various documents in this proceeding. And also the term "maamad bais chayenu".

Could you explain what that term means, "maamad bais chayenu"?

A   Maamad bais chayenu, in the context of these documents clearly means to support the Rebbe, because the term -- the whole context shows that

Jacobs-direct/Shestack

that's what it means.

But the interesting question is why is the Rebbe called of the Rebbe's court, because "bais" means house, and why is the Rebbe and his court called "bais chayenu".

The term "bais chayenu" is found in the traditional sources as meaning the temple.

For example, every Monday and Thursday an orthodox Jew will recite a prayer which says may it be the will of our father in heaven to establish bais chayenu. The term used there is not le'ha-amid, but le'honein, le'honein bais chayenu.

Clearly when this term is used they are thinking of the Rebbe's court as a kind of Temple in miniature.

Actually in the Jewish tradition every synagogue is referred to as a Temple in miniature. But here I don't know of any other group that would use bais chayenu.

Q What is the literal translation of "bais chayenu"?

A Bais chayenu is house of our life.

Q And in the Judaic terms, house of our life,

Jacobs-direct/Shestack

it is the temple?

A   The temple was the house of our life because through the belief that it was true the sacrificial system that the world was kept going.

Q   Now, there was also used in this proceeding the word "pidyon".

Could you differentiate -- first explain what pidyon is, and then differentiate between "pidyon" and "maamad"?

A   Sure.

There is a great difference.

Every Chasid, whether it is Chabad or not, when he visits the Rebbe and asks the Rebbe to pray on his behalf, shall we say, that he should recover from illness or that he should be a better student of the Torah or that he should be able to earn a living or whatever, the procedure is for him to write the petition or somebody to write it for him. And this is called a kvittel. And at the same time he gives a sum of money to the Rebbe.

The rationality of this is he can't expect the Rebbe to pay on his behalf without contributing himself.

And "pidyon", the full term is "pidyon nefesh" which means redemption of the soul, the

Jacobs-direct/Shestack

idea being to contribute to this worthy cause and thereby having a share of what is being achieved, the petitioner is redeeming his soul because he might be a guilty soul and therefore he suffers and therefore he has needs and he redeems it.

Now, that's a personal gift, as it were, if one can put it this way, for services rendered. Of course, the services rendered are spiritual services, and it is payment. And the idea is you don't get anything for nothing and you have to pay for it and you have to redeem your soul by paying for it.

A Chasid who doesn't visit the Rebbe would not give a pidyon because that has no meaning, unless he sent his petition.

Maamad, on the other hand, has a different meaning. Maamad is best compared to membership dues of a learned society or a sacred society, and the dues are expected as token of membership.

Q   Even for a Jew who never goes near the Rebbe?
A   That's right. Although most go to the Rebbe at one time or another. But the point is it is independent of a particular service the Rebbe is

Jacobs-direct/Shestack

rendering for him. It is, rather, that the movement requires support. And how can the movement be supported unless the members pay their dues?

Q Was the gathering of maamad an organized or haphazard? How was it started?

A As far as we can tell it was always organized, although we don't have the terms of organization from the early periods but we can garner that there was an organization of it, as I said before.

Q I would like to direct your attention, for example, to Exhibit 49, which has been previously identified, and ask you if that's one that you had seen before -- excuse me, exhibit 45.

(Handed to the witness.)

A Yes. I have seen that.

MR. HELLERSTEIN: I am sorry, which exhibit is being shown to the witness?

MR. SHESTACK: 45.

Q And what does that show, for example?

A Well, it reads that there are decisions taken with regard to the maamad. And it says that the Agudas Chasidei Chabad decides, the Agudas Chasidei Chabad of America decides to make each member, each

Jacobs-direct/Shestack

person obliged to help the Holy Rebbe Bais Chayenu, which seems to me to mean namely the house of our life, that is, the Rebbe and his court.

And also for the sake of the general work of the community, the amount suggested is -- the target, I suppose it means, would be $10,000 for the year, for the coming year.

The significance of this: It seems to me, is that clearly the appeal for the maamad is for the "Rebbe le'Bais Chayenu". And it goes on to say also for the general work of the movement.

Q Would you also look at Exhibit 49 in connection with, and I direct your attention to page three of the translation of Exhibit 49, and that's in the white book, Plaintiff's Exhibit 49.

A Yes.

Which line of the translation?

Q Page 2. Page 2 and 3.

Are there references there to "maamad" and the use of "maamad"?

A Yes.

MR. HELLERSTEIN: Excuse me, your Honor, may I just have a moment, if your Honor please, before the witness goes on?

THE COURT: Yes.

Jacobs-direct/Shestack

1 (Whereupon, there was a pause in the
2 proceedings.)
3 MR. HELLERSTEIN: Thank you, your Honor.
4 THE COURT: Mr. Shestack or professor,
5 if you get to a point where you might break which
6 is convenient?
7 MR. SHESTACK: This is as convenient as
8 any.
9 THE COURT: Why don't we recess at this
10 point.
11 We will start again in a few minutes.
12
13 (Whereupon, a recess is taken.)
14
15 (Continued on the next page.)

Jacobs-direct/Shestack

517

THE COURT: Before we continue, just on a matter of scheduling, I have another proceeding involving a large number of lawyers and parties about noon or a little after noon.

So, what we will do is take the luncheon recess in your case a little earlier than usual, and in my case it will be a little shorter than usual and break from 12:00 to 1:30.

MR. SHESTACK: Thank you, your Honor.

Q I placed before you, and you have referred to earlier, to Exhibit 45, and I have now placed before you exhibits 40.

Would you now look at Exhibit 39 and Exhibit 38 as well.

(Handed to the witness.)

Q Would you please tell us what the references were to "maamad" in those exhibits and your understanding of those references?

A Well, it seems as clear as can be that the maamad is for the upkeep of the organization. The directorate of the Aguda establish a special committee to arrange the matter of maamad on a fixed basis on an appropriate basis -- this is on page 38.

Q That's Exhibit 38.

Jacobs-direct/Shestack

1 A   Exhibit 38, yes.
2   Exhibit 40 --
3   MR. HELLERSTEIN: Can I have the line
4 number which he was reading, please?
5 Q   Would you refer to the --
6   MR. SHESTACK: If I may identify it,
7 Mr. Hellerstein, it is referring to the third page
8 of the translation.
9 Q   What lines?
10 A   Lines nine to 13. It is the second lines
11 nine to 13.
12   MR. SHESTACK: In Exhibit 40 the witness
13 is referring to the second page of the
14 translation.
15   MR. HELLERSTEIN: I am sorry to
16 interrupt.
17   The witness read something into the
18 record using the word "organization" and I fail to
19 see it.
20   Perhaps I am looking at the wrong page.
21   THE COURT: Mr. Hellerstein you will
22 have an opportunity on cross-examination.
23   THE WITNESS: I am referring to the
24 three passages I am going to read taken together.
25   This is on page 40: All the work on

519
Jacobs-direct/Shestack

behalf of the maamad, the Yeshiva Tomchei Tamimim, is concentrated in the offices of the Aguda where there all the contributions go in and from there are dispersed. Any community or individual in America who sends any sum for the above purposes has to send them to that office or at least to send to that office the receipt that he has received or to inform that office of his contribution.

MR. LEWIN: For the record I think the witness is -- said page 40 and it is Exhibit 40.

A (cont'd) The other one is page 49, the second page, line 6: Further, where it says, the work of Agudas Chabad in the United States and Canada has to concern itself in these areas: One, spreading the study of Chasidus; and two, and so forth; and three, which is the relevent passage to my mind, to establish on a firm basis the support of the yeshivas that are under my direction and to strengthen them in maamadot.

So, clearly the maamadot are to be used at the behest of the Rebbe for not only for his personal use, but to support the yeshivot.

Q You mentioned earlier the use of a word in a historical context, "the rabbi's court."

What do you mean by that or the Rebbe's

Jacobs-direct/Shestack

1 court?
2 A   Well, the rebbes were looked upon by their
3 Chasidim as in a sense royal personages. So
4 the term "court" was used on the analogy of a royal
5 court.
6 Q   Would it --
7 A   It would refer -- the difference between the
8 Court and the organization is this: That the
9 organization is -- that the whole organization,
10 whatever it happens to be, wherever its
11 representatives happen to be situated, the court
12 will be the headquarters of the movement, which was
13 around the Rebbe.
14 Q   Now, would you compare the Chabad
15 organization with philosophies of other Chasidic
16 organizations with respect to accumulation of
17 wealth?
18 A   Yes.
19   It is undoubtedly true that some
20 Chasidic groups believed that it is essential for
21 the Rebbe to be a wealthy man.
22 Q   What is that philosophy called? Is there a
23 term that is used?
24 A   There is no particular term for it, expect
25 that they would refer to the fact -- the rationale

is this, briefly: The Tzadik is -- the Rebbe is thought of in this philosophy, which is not the philosophy of Chabad, and I am talking about Chernobyl for example or Ryzyn.

In these groups you get the kind of mystical idea that the Rebbe is the channel through which the divine grace flows. And, consequently, this spiritual force or energy has to come through the Rebbe to his followers and in a sense to the whole world, granted that philosophy.

Now, the idea would be if the Rebbe is poor, then he only receives a small measure of material goods, precisely because he is poor. And, therefore, there is nothing on which the spiritual force can attach itself. There is nothing to which you can attach yourself.

Consequently, you have to make the Rebbe a rich man. And it has -- he has to have a carriage drawn by white horses and he has to live like a prince and he has to wear gold shoes. And in some branches of this type of attitude the Rebbe would sit on a silver throne or have a huge silver menorah for the festival of Chanukah.

This was based on the idea that the wider the channels, as it were, the more the divine

Jacobs-direct/Shestack

grace can flow through it, for the benefit of mankind and its followers.

This doctrine is not found in Chabad to my knowledge.

To be sure, Chabad would say it is good to support the Rebbe and right to support the Rebbe. And there is nothing in Chabad philosophy that says that a Rebbe can't be rich. But there is no virtue in it.

Whereas, in the other groups there is virtue in the Rebbe being rich. A poor Rebbe would be as it were, a poor Rebbe.

Q What does the word "ashirut" mean?
A Ashirut means wealth.
Q And are the Chasidic groups that you are talking about, do they have that --
A They are made a virtue of ashirut.
Q And in Chabad?
A In Chabad I have never found anything of the sort.
Q There was a reference, and if you would assume this to be correct, Doctor Jacob, in an opening statement to the Court about the Rhyzner [Rishener struck] Rebbe who behaved like a prince.
A Yes.

Jacobs-direct/Shestack

Q   And is that -- could you tell us who the Rhyzner Rebbe is and whether that's a good analogy to Chabad?

A   The Rhyzner was a great grandson of the Magid of Mezeritch, of the organizer of Chasidism as I referred before. His father began what was in some ways a radical departure from Chasidism, because while the Magid and his son were comparatively poor, he believed in the doctrine that we mentioned of "ashirut" and had a court and lived like a Polish count or a Polish prince; and so much so, and this was continued by the Rhyzner and his sons. And so much show that this was a particular course of complaints against the Chasidic movement by those who were opposed to it. They said it was improper, unethical for a Rebbe to live in that style at the expense of his followers who were paying for it.

This is never found in Chabad. And I would say in my understanding of Chabad this would be abhorrent to Chabad.

Now, I have tried to explain why the others have believed in it. I don't believe the Rhyzner, for example, was a particular selfish person or an egotist or a show off, but that was

Jacobs-direct/Shestack

his philosophy.

It wasn't the Chabad philosophy.

Q   Let us turn now to the particular library that is under discussion in this case.

Are you familiar with in general terms with the type of library that Rabbi Joseph Isaac Schneersohn gathered together?

A   I am.

Q   And could you tell the Court the types of books that are found in that library, and with some brief comment by way of identification and types of categories, perhaps?

A   Well, it is clear to me that this library is essentially a research library. It doesn't make any sense as a private library. It certainly doesn't make any sense to me as the private library of a Chasidic Rebbe because it contains such things as runs of learned journals which the Rebbe simply wouldn't have the time to consult, but which scholars would consult.

More particularly --

Q   For example?

A   For example, "hatekufa" or the American learned journals of which there are whole runs and various others.

Jacobs-direct/Shestack

More specifically, there are lots of works, large number of works, perhaps half the library insofar as I could tell -- I can't pretend that I know every shelf in the library -- but as far as I can tell a large number of books are books which the Rebbe would not read but which come to contain opinions which he would consider to be heretical, and which he would strongly discourage his followers from reading.

Q   I would like you to elaborate a little bit on that.

What type of books and why would they be discouraged?

A   For example there is a set of Graetz' History of the Jews, Dubnows history of the Jews.

Graetz was a fierce opponent in his history of Chasidism and has some very nasty things to say. Also Ahad-Ha'am, which is a pseudonym for Asher Ginsberg.

Q   What does "ahad-ha'am" mean?

A   One of the people.

He was a great essayist and it was opposed to -- he was a free thinker, and his views were certainly not at all acceptable in Chasidic circles.

Jacobs-direct/Shestack

There are many copies of things like the prayer book and many copies of the Passover Hagadah, pamphlets --

THE COURT: Can I interrupt?

You refer to the prayer book and other witnesses have as well.

What is the prayer book?

THE WITNESS: The prayer book would be the standard prayer book used by Jews. And, of course, it was printed many times and there were different editions.

Q   Let me stop you there, Doctor Jacobs, and perhaps to elucidate further.

Various groups of Judaism, do they use different types of prayer books?

A   Yes.

Q   And is there a special prayer book that the Chabad uses?

A   Yes.

Q   Is there a Nusach Chabad?

A   It is called Nasach Ari, ha'Ari.

Q   What does that mean?

A   It was Rabbi Isaac Luria, who lived in Safad. He was a great Kabbalist, and the founder of the Lurian Kabbala, as it is called. He lived

Jacobs-direct/Shestack

in the 16th century and he had a certain version of the prayer book which would reflect his understanding of what he called the divine mysteries.

So, the Chabad would use this special prayer book.

But in the library there are any number of copies of different rites, any number of different copies of different rites. And taken together, the heretical material, the Kabbalist material, the New Testament in Hebrew and other Christian works, the learned journals and many prayer books, and so forth, it seems to me that it doesn't make any sense at all to see this as a private library, certainly not a private library of a Chasidic Rebbe. And that it is a research library.

Q Are there antisemetic material?
A Antisemetic material, yes.
Q And communist literature?
A Yes, and the works of Lenin in Hebrew and that kind of thing.
Q From your knowledge of Rabbi Joseph Isaac Schneersohn, were these areas in which he was pursuing research or studying?

Jacobs-direct/Shestack

What can you give us by way of your opinion on that?

A   I would consider that to be extremely unlikely.

Q   Why is that?

A   Because the leaders of the movement from the beginning were hostile to this kind of literature. They were hostile to any kind of literature which was not, in quotes, sacred.

Q   Why does someone gather a lot of varied editions and a lot of copies and other versions? What is the purpose of that?

MR. HELLERSTEIN: I object to the question.

The witness has not been qualified --

MR. SHESTACK: I withdraw the question.

Q   In your opinion, is this the kind of a library that a rabbi might have gathered, the Rebbe might have gathered for his own personal glory or reputation?

MR. HELLERSTEIN: Again, your Honor, I object.

The witness is asked to speculate. There is no showing that he made any showing of his own on Rabbi Joseph I. Schneersohn and is competent

Jacobs-direct/Shestack

1 enough to answer the question.
2   THE COURT: I take it this is whether
3 the possession of this would add renown to the
4 possessor, whether he was the 6th Rebbe or someone
5 else.
6   Could you answer it in those terms?
7   THE WITNESS: Yes.
8   It is clearly, as I have seen it, a
9 library that only makes sense if it is for the
10 prestige of someone or some organization.
11   MR. HELLERSTEIN: Again, your Honor, I
12 object and move to strike.
13   The witness is speculating on the basis
14 of books he has seen and not on the basis of any
15 study that he has made. He has not been qualified
16 as an expert on libraries. He has not been
17 qualified as an expert on the lives of Joseph I.
18 Schneersohn. His expertise is on the subject of
19 philosophy and thesiology and Talmudic discipline.
20   Your Honor, this particular question is
21 asking for a speculation.
22   THE COURT: Do you have a library
23 yourself?
24   THE WITNESS: Yes, I do.
25   May I say that the question of expertise

Jacobs-direct/Shestack

is relevant in that one has a knowledge of the kind of things that a Chasidic Rebbe would study and one can draw conclusions therefore on the issues in the library.

I am not speculating on Rabbi Joseph Yitzchok.

MR. HELLERSTEIN: Shall I comment?

THE COURT: I will deny the application to strike.

If you wish to inquire further into the witness' acquaintance with other research libraries, you can certainly do that.

I take it as a scholar you have had occasion to consult research libraries?

THE WITNESS: Yes.

THE COURT: In the various places you have studied?

THE WITNESS: Yes.

THE COURT: Go ahead.

Q To perhaps clarify a little bit, you are familiar with the Chabad philosophy as expounded by various Chabad rebbes, including Rabbi Joseph Schneersohn?

A Yes.

Q And you have read his works in Ma'amorim?

Jacobs-direct/Shestack

1 A   Yes, something like that.
2 Q   Based on your knowledge of Chabad philosophy,
3 is it consistent with that philosophy for a Rebbe
4 to gather a personal library of the nature of the
5 one involved here, and if -- could you tell us what
6 is consistent with Chabad philosophy in so far as
7 you know, addressing yourself to the purposes that
8 such a library might serve?
9   MR. HELLERSTEIN: I object first to the
10 form of the question.
11   THE COURT: I sustain the objection to
12 form.
13   MR. SHESTACK: I will rephrase the
14 question.
15 Q   Can you relate the acquisition of a library
16 of this kind to Chabad philosophy?
17 A   Consider the --
18   MR. HELLERSTEIN: Objection as
19 irrelevant.
20   What we are asking about is a particular
21 application and not in terms of the philosophic
22 speculation having to do with the philosophy of
23 Chabad.
24   MR. SHESTACK: Your Honor, if I may
25 answer --

Jacobs-direct/Shestack

THE COURT: I don't think you need to respond. I think what it requires is simply a prefatory question.

Are you able to draw any conclusions as to the relationship between the particular texts that you have had an opportunity to examine and what you know about Chasidic philosophy in general? Do you have an opinion that there is or is not some relationship or not?

THE WITNESS: There is no relationship whatsoever to many of the books in the library and Chasidic philosophy.

In fact, many of the books are opposed to Chasidic philosophy.

Q   Is there anything in Chasidic philosophy which would explain why a library of this sort has been put together or not?

THE WITNESS: It is an innovation, no doubt about that. And I can only assume that this it was put together as a research library for the benefit of scholars.

MR. HELLERSTEIN: I object to the last part and move to strike what follows, "I assume."

THE COURT: The application is denied.

Does Chasidic philosophy take any

Jacobs-direct/Shestack

position with regard to scholarship and research or not?

THE WITNESS: In more recent years it has taken into account the findings of scholars and it would seek to encourage scholarship.

I would frankly say that to me the whole library, granted its contents, its contents is very strange for a Chasidic Rebbe to have.

Q Doctor Jacob, based on your examination of the kind of books that are found in this library, and based on your knowledge of Chabad philosophy as well as your knowledge of the activities and philosophies of Chabad that was founded by Rabbi Joseph Schneersohn do you have an opinion on the basis that this library was acquired?

MR. HELLERSTEIN: I don't believe the conclusion in the question follows from the premise in the question, your Honor. I move to strike it.

THE COURT: Objection overruled.

Do you have an opinion on that subject or not?

THE WITNESS: Yes.

THE COURT: Would you express it.

Q Would you give us your opinion?

A It seems to me the only way this library

Jacobs-direct/Shestack

makes sense is to encourage research, and that means that there is an appreciation of the value of objective research. But that also means that it's a research library, and I could only make real sense of it, if this were considered to be an institution that should be there, since in the modern world --

MR. HELLERSTEIN: Excuse me, your Honor.

The witness has answered the question and is now expressing what he would like to see happen.

THE COURT: Overruled.

Go ahead.

Q Continue.

A It only makes sense to me if this is done for someone or something, some institutions prestige -- there if I may say so with whatever expertise I have that does come in, I can't imagine a Chasidic Rebbe or Lubavitch Rebbe doing something of that sort at the expense of his followers for his personal prestige. This would be contrary to the whole concept of Chabad.

And if it were done for prestige it would be the prestige of the movement. Otherwise I

Jacobs-direct/Shestack

can't make any sense of it at all.

Q Doctor Jacobs, based on your knowledge of maamad and Chabad doctrine, do you have an opinion as to whether or not it is consistent with Chabad philosophy for Rabbi Joseph I. Schneersohn to use maamad funds to acquire a rather large personal library such as the one involved here?

MR. HELLERSTEIN: Objection to the form of the question.

I think there are two questions there. One is whether he would use maamad funds to acquire a library, and the second is whether it would be used to acquire this kind of library.

THE COURT: Overruled.

You can answer the question.

THE WITNESS: I am sure the Rebbe could use funds to acquire a library, if by library is meant the books that every rabbi needs like the Talmud and the codes, and Responsa, and the Chasidic literature.

I can't imagine a Rebbe acquiring this kind of library, which, as we said, contains material which by no stretch of the imagination could be considered a personal library for the Rebbe's personal use.

Jacobs-direct/Shestack

So, I would say, if then it is for prestige it can only be the prestige of the movement.

I can't imagine a Rebbe, to put it bluntly, what we are saying the Rebbe may acquire this library in order to increase his personal prestige. This is not a sort of thing a Rebbe does or a Rebbe should do.

So, although anything is possible, but from my knowledge of not Rabbi Joseph Yitchok particularly, but what Chabad has been teaching over the many years, it seems inconceivable to me that a Rebbe would do this to increase his personal prestige any more than he would buy splendid paintings or tapestries in order to increase his personal prestige and if he did that, and if he didn't -- if he did that it would be so the headquarters of the community should be resplendent.

(Continued on the next page.)

```
                                                        537
                        Jacobs-direct-Shestack
1   EXAMINATION CONTINUES
2   BY MR. SHESTACK:
3   Q      Dr. Jacobs, I invite your attention to
4   exhibit 316-A and ask you to examine that document.
5              (Handing to the witness.)
6   A      The Rebbe is stating his needs.
7   Q      Wait.  Just examine it.
8   A      Yes.
9   Q      Give everyone else a chance to find that.
10  A      Shall I translate it?
11  Q      I direct you --
12             MR. HELLERSTEIN:  Excuse me one minute, if
13  Your Honor please.
14             We don't have a translation of 316-A.
15             MR. LEWIN:  As its number indicates, Your
16  Honor, it was inserted late in this group and even in
17  the most recent effort to translate every document in
18  this series, frankly, it was overlooked until this
19  morning.
20             THE COURT:  Do you have a --
21             MR. LEWIN:  We will provide a
22  translation.  I understand Mr. Shestack wants to
23  refer to one particular paragraph and --
24             MR. SHESTACK:  I'll ask the witness --
25             MR. HELLERSTEIN:  Excuse me.
```

Jacobs-direct-Shestack

Your Honor, I object.

I will not be able to deal in any kind of a cross-examination without knowing the context that anything is requested of Dr. Jacobs to answer. It simply seems to me unfair to subject me to the use of a document and language that I am not familiar with, at least not sufficiently to profound any kind of question or understanding of context.

MR. SHESTACK: Your Honor --

THE COURT: How do you know until we've had this translated, the question asked and answered? If you find yourself devastated by it, we can take a -- give you sometime to cross-examine on the subject later or it can be stricken.

Let's --

MR. SHESTACK: During the cross-examination -- probably won't take place until after luncheon break. Barry Gourary can certainly translate it and the witness here will translate it too.

MR. HELLERSTEIN: Excuse me.

I don't think it fair. If Your Honor wishes additional comment, to subject my client, during the luncheon break, when I need -- I have need of his consultation for other purposes, to be busy

Jacobs-direct-Shestack

1 translating a particular document,. It is the
2 obligation of counsel to supply me with translations
3 beforehand.
4 Nor am I able to intelligently to
5 object, nor am I able to intelligently to evaluate
6 what is requested, nor am I able to intelligently to
7 fit any questions with regard to this document into a
8 total plan of cross-examination.
9 The witness is here for days, not
10 here --
11 MR. SHESTACK: Your Honor, I have an
12 idea. May I suggest this? I don't want to do
13 anything that interferes with Mr. Hellerstein's
14 intelligent operation. I'll have the witness
15 translate it, not ask questions about it. Then ask
16 questions about it after the recess.
17 Would that be satisfactory?
18 THE COURT: All right. Why don't you do
19 that?
20 EXAMINATION CONTINUES
21 BY MR. SHESTACK:
22 Q   Dr. Jacobson, addressing the second full
23 paragraph, starts with the Hebrew word -- starting
24 with the first full paragraph on the -- on the page.
25 MR. HELLERSTEIN: Your Honor, if Your

Jacobs-direct-Shestack

Honor please, I thought Mr. Shestack was deferring questions until after the recess so I would have the opportunity --

MR. SHESTACK: Just to translate it.

THE COURT: Just a translation, to get things started.

THE WITNESS: You want me to --

MR. HELLERSTEIN: I object, Your Honor.

THE COURT: The objection is overruled.

Go ahead.

EXAMINATION CONTINUES
BY MR. SHESTACK:

Q   Start with that second paragraph.

THE COURT: Just translate the terms. If it is appropriate to strike the translation, I will entertain the application after I have heard it and you have heard it.

Go ahead.

MR. HELLERSTEIN: May I know what is being translated?

MR. LEWIN: Second paragraph.

THE WITNESS: For my personal residence, about five rooms would be sufficient but if it is essential that there be a room suitable for a place of prayer for the regular minyan, three times a day,

Jacobs-direct-Shestack

and where one can study the Torah there and another room near to it that would also a connection with the minyan and a room, another room for the bureau, the office, and for the library, so that the total would be about ten spacious rooms.

Q   You translated the word "bureau" from the Hebrew. What does the word "bureau" mean?

A   Bureau is the word bureau, French, from the French. That means -- it is a word they used in Russia for office, I believe.

MR. SHESTACK: For the record, this is a letter from Riga by Rebbe Schneur Zalman in Riga.

Will Your Honor indulge me for one minute?

THE COURT: Go ahead.

EXAMINATION CONTINUES

BY MR. SHESTACK:

Q   I'd like to show you and English translation of what has been marked as Exhibit 438.

MR. LEWIN: Your Honor, that's a translation we gave Your Honor at the end of the session yesterday.

THE COURT: Okay.

MR. LEWIN: Would Your Honor like another copy?

Jacobs-direct-Shestack

1 THE COURT: No. I've got it right here.
2 All right. What is the question?
3 MR. SHESTACK: I just marked, brought it
4 to his attention.
5 EXAMINATION CONTINUES
6 BY MR. SHESTACK:
7 Q Have you seen that letter before?
8 A Yes.
9 Q And could you briefly just summarize the
10 contents of that letter before I ask you the --
11 A It is a letter to renowned --
12 MR. HELLERSTEIN: I object to the form of
13 the question, Your Honor.
14 THE COURT: Overruled.
15 A (Continuing) It is a letter to the renowned scholar
16 Dr. Alexander Marx, who was the librarian of the
17 Jewish Theological Seminary, and it is asking him to
18 use his influence to rescue the library which was
19 seized by the Nazis in Poland in 1939.
20 Then it gives a description of the
21 material.
22 Q Now --
23 A Yes.
24 Q Now, if you will look at the fourth paragraph,
25 is that -- what is the reference in that fourth

Jacobs-direct-Shestack

1 paragraph?
2 A   It says, there are books, several thousand
3 books, among them many ancient books, great volume,
4 very rare. These books are the property of Agudas
5 Chasidei Chabad of America and Canada.
6 Q   In your -- with your knowledge of philosophy of
7 a -- of Rabbi Joseph Schneersohn, would you have any
8 reason to come to doubt the Rabbi's belief in the
9 accuracy of that statement, if he said that in a
10 letter to Dr. Mark?
11   MR. HELLERSTEIN: May I hear the question,
12 please?
13   THE COURT: What?
14   MR. HELLERSTEIN: May I hear the question
15 again?
16   THE COURT: If you are going to object to
17 it, I will sustain an objection.
18   MR. HELLERSTEIN: Yes.
19   THE COURT: I don't think it is very
20 helpful just to have a yes or no to that.
21   Could you reframe the question or
22 perhaps I can.
23   Is there anything you know about
24 Chasidic philosophy or philosophy of this particular
25 movement in particular which would legitimize, if

Jacobs-direct-Shestack

that is the appropriate word, a statement by the rabbi that was a misstatement, a knowing misstatement, whether these books or -- were property of this organization or not?

THE WITNESS: I can't see the purpose of it unless it --

THE COURT: Are there any circumstances within the philosophy which would explain an intentional misstatement in a letter of this sort?

THE WITNESS: Intentional misstatement which is sort of -- another word for a deliberate lie, would only be tolerated in the Jewish tradition and we're not talking about Chasidic tradition, but Jewish tradition generally, in the direst of circumstances, such as to save life.

THE COURT: All right.

THE WITNESS: Or possibly to save -- to save a property of religious value that was going to be destroyed immediately.

I don't see that this -- that there is anything that would justify it.

Q   When was this letter written?

MR. HELLERSTEIN: Move to strike the last part, which is the observation, which is not responsive to Your Honor's question.

Jacobs-direct-Shestack

THE COURT: Overruled.

Q When was this letter written?

A When was this letter written? The letter was written in 24 of Adar, the first, 5706, which is 1946.

Q In your opinion, were there any dire circumstances at that time that would justify a misstatement of fact of this nature?

MR. HELLERSTEIN: I object, unless there is --

THE COURT: I will sustain an objection to that particular question, since it seems to require a rather concrete set of circumstances.

All right. Go ahead.

Q Under Jewish law, if you do make a misstatement in -- under circumstances where you're trying to save life or property, what are you required to do?

A You're required to make a declaration in the presence of two witnesses that you are making it under duress.

Q You see any such statement in this document?

MR. HELLERSTEIN: I object to the form of the question.

MR. SHESTACK: It is obvious.

I withdraw it.

Jacobs-direct-Shestack

1 THE COURT: All right.
2 MR. SHESTACK: Your Honor, I think that
3 you will take judicial notice of the fact that 1946
4 was after the war. The Nazis were conquered and the
5 territories were under the control of the Allied
6 Forces.
7 THE COURT: Well, I will take judicial
8 notice of the first two. I don't know what
9 territories you have in mind.
10 At all events, let's go ahead.
11 MR. SHESTACK: I think I'm almost through,
12 Your Honor.
13 You may cross-examine.
14 THE COURT: All right. Do you want to
15 begin, Mr. Hellerstein?
16 MR. HELLERSTEIN: I'd like to take about
17 ten or 15 minutes and use it profitably, Your Honor.
18 CROSS-EXAMINATION
19 BY MR. HELLERSTEIN:
20 Q Dr. Jacobson, you may still have Exhibit 428 in
21 front of you?
22 A 438?
23 Q Yes.
24 It is the document that Mr. Shestack was
25 just examining you about?

Jacobs-direct-Shestack

1 A   Oh, yes. The letter to Alexander Marx.
2 Q   Yes.
3 A   Yes, I have that.
4 Q   If you like, there is Hebrew version just next
5 to it.
6 A   Yes.
7 Q   If -- you could consult either one.
8   Let's look at the first paragraph. Line
9 three in the English translation makes reference to
10 ancient manuscripts and valuable books which have
11 been kept in my library in Otwock.
12   Looking at the Hebrew, do you have any
13 doubt that "my library" is correct?
14 A   It would depend on what you mean by "my,"
15 because the Hebrew says specific, be-sifriah she-li.
16 Q   Is --
17 A   Sifriah she-li means -- the word library in
18 English as in Hebrew can mean the books, it can mean
19 the place and I -- I read it as being the place. The
20 books that are in my -- in my library, namely in the
21 room, my study, the room I use as a library.
22 Q   She-li means mine?
23 A   She-li means mine, but the sifriah is --
24 sifriah she-li, my -- in my study.
25 Q   Later on in that paragraph, looking at English

Jacobs-direct-Shestack

1 version, Rabbi Schneersohn says that the manuscripts,
2 books besides others added later were the personal
3 library of the well-known Shmuel Wiener.
4   Have you come across the name Shmuel
5 Wiener in your studies?
6 A   Yes.
7   THE COURT: All right.
8   (Continued on next page.).

Jacobs-cross/Hellerstein

1 Q   Was he the custodian or the librarian, of the
2 oriental library in the Leningrad Museum?
3 A   Yes.
4 Q   And this is a reference, as you understand
5 it, to a purchase of Rabbi Schneersohn of the
6 personal library of Mr. Wiener?
7 A   Yes.
8 Q   And he said I once bought it, does he not?
9 A   Which line is that?
10 Q   The last phrase in the paragraph?
11 A   The last phrase in paragraph two?
12 A   Yes.
13   MR. HELLERSTEIN: May I approach to
14 point out the line?
15 A   Yes.
16 Q   So, it is the last phrase of the first
17 paragraph.
18 A   Yes.
19 Q   And the word there, "I once bought it", is
20 the Hebrew words, and pardon my enunciation,
21 "kaniti"?
22 A   Kaniti.
23 Q   And that means I bought it?
24 A   Yes.
25 Q   And the suffix, roughly, T I --

Jacobs-cross/Hellerstein

A   Not necessarily.

Because it means exactly the same as the English, I applied it. It doesn't necessarily mean that I acquired it, doesn't mean my property. The word "kaniti", I could have bought something on behalf of someone else and it still means "kaniti".

Q   And do you see anything here to suggest that he bought it for someone else?

A   Not from that paragraph, but from the letter as a whole I would say yes.

Q   And who else? Who would it be that he bought it for?

A   He bought it for Agudas Chasidei Chabad.

Q   Where, in Israel? In Russia? Poland? England? France?

A   America and Canada.

Q   The U.S. and Canada?

A   Yes.

He said these books are the property of Agudas Chasidei Chabad of America and Canada.

Q   Under Halacha, if someone is buying as an agent for someone else is it customary to have some kind of written authorization?

A   Well, that would depend. There is such a thing as assumed, an assumed ability to act on

Jacobs-cross/Hellerstein

1 someone's behalf.
2 Q   Where were these books stored between 1925
3 and 1940 when Rabbi Schneersohn came to this
4 country? Do you know?
5 A   I don't know.
6 Q   And he goes on and says, speaking about
7 manuscripts, in the third paragraph, the
8 manuscripts are registered under the names of the
9 rabbis, members of Agudas Chasidei Chabad, and he
10 named several. And he says who are the official
11 owners of his property.
12   Under Jewish law how do they show their
13 official ownership?
14 A   I don't follow.
15 Q   How does one follow the official ownership in
16 one self if the property is in the custody of
17 someone else?
18 A   I still don't follow you.
19   Do you mean --
20 Q   Let's say, Doctor Jacobs, that you are the
21 owner of some valuable manuscripts and I have been
22 holding them for some fifteen years. How do you
23 show to the outside world that you are the owner?
24 A   There are various ways.
25   One would be to produce witnesses that

Jacobs-cross/Hellerstein

they show, and another one would be to produce permission that the one who is holding it is holding it for me, that he has admitted holding it for me.

Q   In the course of the fifteen years that this has accumulated would you look for some declaration of witnesses on the part of some so-called registered owners or instructions given to the so-called custodian or some other form of writing which would show evidence of a distant person ownership?

A   How would I know that?

Q   What would you look for under Halacha if you were looking for evidence of ownership?

A   I would look for some kind of evidence of ownership. But it would depend. In Jewish law, as far as I know in any other system as well, I don't have to have evidence of ownership that this jacket I am wearing is mine.

Q   Because you are wearing it, it is in custody?

A   Or my cupboards or library.

Q   But if the manuscripts were in the custody of someone else for a long period of time, would it make a difference?

A   It would depend how one had viewed it at that

Jacobs-cross/Hellerstein

1 time.
2   THE COURT: Excuse me, the term which
3 has been translated here as registered, first of
4 all is that an accurate translation.
5   THE WITNESS: Well, the Hebrew is
6 "ri'shumim", and registered is not a bad
7 translation, it is not an inaccurate translation,
8 the root "re'shum" means to mark.
9   So, the word means are marked. It is
10 not registered in the sense of a sort of formal
11 document or with that kind of a stamp as the word
12 register might suggest in English.
13 Q Is there any --
14   THE COURT: Excuse me, just a moment.
15   MR. HELLERSTEIN: I am sorry.
16   THE WITNESS: "Ri'shumim" means they are
17 noted, they are marked.
18   THE COURT: Within the area of your
19 expertise, and I think this maybe the question that
20 you were being asked by the attorney, but is there
21 any particular place based on your expertise where
22 you have looked for these marks or not?
23 A I wouldn't know that. It is not -- the
24 reference is not, in so far as I can see as in an
25 official office that these are registered.

Jacobs-cross/Hellerstein

THE COURT: Not necessarily?

THE WITNESS: They are --

THE COURT: In other words, would you head for the town hall? Would you open up the book itself to look inside?

THE WITNESS: No.

I would imagine that it means that somewhere there is a record.

THE COURT: Okay.

Q You said you had seen this letter before. When you examined it were you shown any record?

A No.

Q Did you ask to see any record?

A No.

Q Did you ask to see these particular manuscripts?

A No.

Q Now, this was written in 1946. Possibly some of these registered owners would have died in the meantime.

Would you have asked if any of their heirs are now official owners of the property?

THE COURT: Excuse me.

I don't quite understand the question.

Jacobs-cross/Hellerstein

1 Perhaps I wouldn't understand the answer.
2   MR. HELLERSTEIN: I am sorry, I will
3 reword it.
4 Q   There is a reference here with regard to the
5 manuscripts, to several named rabbis, Rabbi Israel
6 Jacobson, his son-in-law, Rabbi Shlomo Zalman
7 Hecht, two people.
8 A   Yes.
9 Q   And they are said to be the official owners
10 of the property.
11 A   Yes.
12 Q   And if you wanted to know who the official
13 owners were in these -- and these two gentlemen had
14 in the meantime died, who would now be the official
15 owners under Jewish law?
16 A   Who would be the official owners?
17 Q   Would it be the heirs of these two people?
18 A   Would be the heir of these two people.
19 Q   So whether it was a manuscript owned by Rabbi
20 Joseph I. Schneersohn or a manuscript owned by
21 Rabbi Israel Jacobson or Rabbi Shlomo Zalman Hecht,
22 the ownership would be private?
23 A   You mean private to these rabbis?
24 Q   Yes, or their heirs?
25 A   Yes.

Jacobs-cross/Hellerstein

Q   And not the property of Agudas Chasidei Chabad of the United States or Canada?

A   I don't know about that.

I mean you are asking me something about which I have no expertise whatsoever. I am merely interpreting a letter here.

It seems to me, and I would say it seems to everyone who reads this letter that they are registered under the names of these rabbis who are members of Agudas Chasidei Chabad. If it is a private -- if he is saying that they belong privately to these rabbis, why mention members of the Agudas Chasidei Chabad?

THE COURT: If I can interrupt again, the phrase that is interpreted here as "the official owners," first of all is that a fair and accurate interpretation.

THE WITNESS: The word used is, it has "rishamim" as the adjective and it really means it should be strictly speaking if it is translated as registered in the first line of the paragraph, it should be translated as the registered owners of this property. It is the same word.

THE COURT: I see.

Q   So, you would look for some marking to show

Jacobs-cross/Hellerstein

1 their registration of ownership?
2 A   Yes.
3 Q   And the inference of that marking is that the
4 people who made the marking or caused the marking
5 to be made would be the owners?
6 A   Would be the owners acting on behalf of
7 Agudas Chasidei Chabad is how I understand it.
8 Q   Do they say acting or members?
9 A   Why mention members of Agudas Chasidei Chabad
10 then? Because if it means certain manuscripts are
11 registered by -- to certain members, then it would
12 be irrelevant that they are members of Agudas
13 Chasidei Chabad. I can't see any other
14 interpretation of that.
15   Whatever expertise I have on Jewish
16 mysticism doesn't give me expertise on the
17 explanation of a particular paragraph.
18 Q   Particularly when the next paragraph the
19 mention of the books is to the property of Agudas
20 Chasidei Chabad of America and Canada, without
21 mentioning of individuals?
22 A   Yes.
23 Q   It would be right then if Rabbi Schneersohn
24 wants to remark about ownership is in Agudas
25 Chasidei Chabad he could do it, and when he wanted

Jacobs-cross/Hellerstein

to remark about ownership of individuals he could do that also?

A   It could.

But it seems to me what is happening here in the Hebrew is that the words for property, these words for property, a different word is used from before, the word used before is "rechush", these books are the property, "rechush" of Agudas Chasidei Chabad.

So, what he seems to be saying the books, thousands of them are the property of Agudas Chasidei Chabad, without referring to individuals in the other things he is saying that they are owners or representitives of Agudas Chasidei Chabad and he mentions their names, otherwise why say members of Agudas Chasidei Chabad.

Q   Is there a word for representatives in Hebrew?

A   Yes, "shlichim".

Q   Was it used?

A   No.

But I would say it is understood as registered under the names of, and members of Agudas Chasidei Chabad.

Supposing they belong to a Zionist

Jacobs-cross/Hellerstein

1 society. Would you say members of the Bronx
2 Zionist Society? It wouldn't be relevant.
3 Q Perhaps if you wanted to describe a person.
4   We really don't know, do we, looking at
5 this letter, what Rabbi Schneersohn had in mind, do
6 we?
7 A We have a fair idea what he had in mind, I
8 would have thought.
9 Q Let me ask you one more question before the
10 lunch break.
11   In the third paragraph, again using the
12 English translation, the official owners of this
13 property, is the word owners plural or singular in
14 the Hebrew?
15 A It is in the plural.
16   MR. HELLERSTEIN: We can break here,
17 your Honor.
18   THE WITNESS: Can I say something which
19 is very important?
20 Q Yes.
21 A In Hebrew you always talk about ownership in
22 the plural. The words "ba'alim", you never find it
23 in the singular. You say the owner pays. You
24 don't say the owner pays "ha'baal". You say
25 "ha'ba'alim". In the bible you say, "la'gag

Jacobs-cross/Hellerstein

1 ba'alav ve'lo mi'shaleim." The law code in
2 Exodous. The plural is always used in --
3 Q   Repeat that phrase?
4 A   La'gag ba'alav ve'lo mi'shaleim. It doesn't
5 say "ba'aloe", "ba'alav".
6 Q   "Ba'alav" is not singular?
7 A   No plural.
8 Q   Do you find any reference to "ba'alav"?
9 A   No, "ba'alim". That's how you write in
10 Hebrew.
11   THE COURT: We will take the luncheon
12 recess and we will start at 1:30.
13   MR. SHESTACK: Do you want the tables
14 cleared for the proceeding?
15   THE COURT: There will be quite a few
16 people here. So, I am afraid that you have to put
17 it in the jury box.
18
19   (Luncheon recess.)

Jacobs-cross-Hellerstein

                    A F T E R N O O N   S E S S I O N.
THE COURT: All right.
MR. LEWIN: May I just raise one preliminary matter, Your Honor? I'm sorry.
THE COURT: Yes.
MR. LEWIN: As Mr. Hellerstein knows, I advised him, during the lunch recess, some member of the audience, who was here and just heard the testimony this morning on the subject of maamad approached me with some information which I think makes him a relevant witness. I had not known about his existence or about the potential testimony prior to the lunch break and consequently, he was not on our witness list.

We'd like to be able to call him and Mr. Hellerstein said I would have to apply to Your Honor. He would not consent. Simply in discussions between us. He's been omitted from the witness list and as I say --

THE COURT: Have you given your adversary the name at this point?

MR. LEWIN: I have told him the content. I am perfectly prepared to tell him the name of the witness. Benjamin Levitan is his name.

THE COURT: All right. Have you told the

Jacobs-cross-Hellerstein

1 witness --
2   MR. LEWIN: I have told --
3   THE COURT: He'd better leave if he's
4 going --
5   MR. LEWIN: Yes.
6   THE COURT: Comply with the exclusion
7 rule?
8   MR. LEWIN: Yes, I have told him.
9   MR. COGAN: Your Honor, in -- this is not
10 the first additonal information that's come to light
11 since the trial started. Mr. Lewin today handed me
12 two letters that had come in from someone listening
13 in the audience and we're concerned about this
14 constant increase of information over which we've had
15 no discovery. We think that's the purpose of the
16 witness and exhibit lists and indeed when we asked
17 for an additional two weeks to prepare for trial,
18 three weeks ago, Mr. --
19   THE COURT: When we get to this witness'
20 testimony, if after we have heard other witnesses it
21 is really necessary to hear it, I'll consider whether
22 there was diligence in discovering this witness or in
23 failing to discover the witness earlier. But at
24 least you know who the person is and the person is
25 unfortunately not going to be able to hear the rest

                                                              563
                          Jacobs-cross-Hellerstein

1   of the trial.
2   All right. Go ahead.
3   EXAMINATION CONTINUES
4   BY MR. HELLERSTEIN:
5   Q   Dr. Jacobs, I think you mention --
6   THE COURT: Mr. Hellerstein, I'd prefer if
7   you could be over here. The reason is it gets to be
8   like a tennis game when someone is on this side and
9   someone over here (indicating).
10   If you could maybe put it alongside the
11 jury rail?
12   MR. HELLERSTEIN: I wanted to be closer to
13 my guiders.
14   THE COURT: They can join you over there.
15 If you'd like to, take a seat in the jury box.
16   MR. COGAN: You don't mind my walking over
17 there if I have anything to say?
18   THE COURT: No. Have a seat in the jury
19 box, if you'd prefer. That would be fine.
20   MR. COGAN: Okay.
21 Q   Dr. Jacobs, you have mentioned that you knew
22 some of the contents of the library of Rabbi Joseph
23 I. Schneersohn. When did you first, if any time, see
24 the books in his library?
25 A   The first time I saw the books was last night.

Jacobs-cross-Hellerstein

1 I am not a resident of the United States.
2 Q   I understand.
3 A   I knew of the library. But the first time I
4 had an opportunity of seeing it was last night.
5 Q   When did you first know of the library?
6 A   I don't recall.
7 Q   Long time ago?
8 A   Long time ago.
9 Q   When you visited the library last night, what
10 time was it, approximately?
11 A   It was about 6:00 o'clock, I believe.
12 Q   And in a research library, around 6:00 o'clock,
13 is that a time of use by scholars?
14 A   It would depend. In my country, the answer
15 would be no. But I gather in the United States the
16 answer would be yes.
17 Q   Did you see any carrels or desks where a
18 scholar might sit down and take out a book and read
19 it for a while?
20 A   No. Because it seems to be under a state of
21 repair.
22 Q   It seemed to be?
23 A   Under a state of repair. Dust and so on.
24 Obviously something had been repaired. But I don't
25 know whether that was the reason.

1   The answer, simple answer is no.
2 Q No.
3   Do you know if at any time there were
4 carrels or desks for people to sit down and study?
5 A How would I know that?
6 Q I assume the answer is no?
7 A The answer is, I don't know.
8 Q Yes.
9   And did you see any card catalog?
10 A No.
11 Q Have you seen --
12 A I have seen a catalog. Not a card catalog.
13 Q Have you seen a list of all the books in the
14 library?
15 A Listing of the books, yes.
16 Q Do you know when it was prepared?
17 A No.
18 Q Do you know if there had been a listing
19 existing, say, ten years?
20 A No.
21 Q Do you know when the last time -- when was the
22 last time that a book was put into that library?
23 A No.
24   How would I know this information?
25 Q I don't know. I'm just asking.

Jacobs-cross-Hellerstein

1 Q   Did you see any students in the
2 library? Any yeshiva students, for example?
3 A   It was a -- the library was closed at the
4 time.
5 Q   And do you know that as a matter of fact, the
6 library has always been a closed library?
7 A   I don't know that.
8 Q   Have you ever come across a research library
9 that was a closed library?
10 A   If you mean research library to which access is
11 sometimes difficult, the answer is yes.
12 Q   What do you mean by access difficulty?
13 A   Well, I've known research libraries where you
14 have to get special permission to consult the books.
15 And it is locked, for example, against vandals and
16 theft.
17 Q   And do you know if over the course of years
18 people obtained permission to view the books in the
19 library? In this library?
20 A   No. I am unaware.
21 Q   You didn't see anybody in the library doing
22 research in any manner?
23 A   No.
24 Q   Have you ever come across a researcher who used
25 this particular library for research?

Jacobs-cross-Hellerstein

A   I have seen it referred to in -- in research works.

Q   And you have seen it referred to as a library containing lots of rich material in Chasidus. Have you met anyone who actually penetrated the library and researched in it?

A   If you mean by met, I have seen in writing that people have used the library, scholars have used the library.

THE COURT: Excuse me. What sort of references have you seen in research works?

THE WITNESS: Well, in bibliographies of Chasidic books, I have seen references to the -- to the Lubavitch library.

THE COURT: As a library that exists or in terms of particular books that are available in the library?

THE WITNESS: I don't follow Your Honor.

THE COURT: In a bibliography, I assume this is a listing of books and I just wanted to know whether there was a reference to the library in general or a reference to a particular book which --

THE WITNESS: The reference to particular books to be found in this library.

THE COURT: Okay.

Jacobs-cross-Hellerstein

1 Do you recall what the research was that
2 you saw that had this reference?
3 THE WITNESS: No, I can't say that. I
4 have seen it over the years, in -- referred to as
5 Lubavitch Library.
6 THE COURT: Okay. Go ahead.
7 Q Has that been the way you have seen it, as a
8 Lubavitch Library?
9 A You mean, hitherto?
10 Q Yes, hitherto?
11 A It is hard to answer that because it was -- it
12 was quite peripheral, frankly. The whole -- I knew
13 there were -- it was a library among libraries, but
14 it didn't particularly come into my purview, as it
15 were.
16 Q You were a student of Chasidus, were you not?
17 A Yes.
18 Q Are you not? You still are?
19 A Yes.
20 Q And in particular, you say you are a student of
21 Chabad?
22 A Yes.
23 Q Would it have been useful to your purposes to
24 have been able to spend time in this library?
25 A Well, the simple answer to that is I don't live

in the United States. It would be difficult. I've got access in London to equally comprehensive libraries, so there was no need for me to do this.

Q   You have been to the United States before today?

A   I should add, I should add to this, that there has been a great deal of publishing by the Agudas Chabad so that most of the stuff that's required, most of the stuff I required for my research is available in copy -- photocopy.

Q   The --

A   So there was no occasion when I had to consult, shall we say, a rare manuscript.

When I translated my work Tract on Ecstasy on the middle Rebbe, I was fortunate enough to have access to what most scholars considered to be the Rebbe's actual autograph, so the answer to your question is, it just never happened, that I had to consult this library.

Q   You've been in the United States as a visiting professor over the years, have you not?

A   Yes.

Q   And were you lecturing on Chabad among other things?

A   Yes.

Jacobs-cross-Hellerstein

Q And would it have been extremely inconvenient to have spent some time in this library? While you were here in the United States?

A It wouldn't have been terribly convenient. There was no reason for me to do so.

Q I see.

A I mean, you know, if I may just elaborate? I'm -- I'm -- I was certainly not aware, nor am I aware now that the only way one can do research into Chabad is to consult this library. There are excellent libraries which contain a host -- the British Museum Library in London, host of works, and all that I needed.

Q So this library is not unique in that sense?

A I wouldn't know that.

Q Would you like to know that? Would you want to know if there was a particular say manuscript of the second Lubavitch Rebbe for you to consult?

A I'm sure in that that respect it must be unique. I would imagine so. Because they have the document, the original document.

Q Your professors or teachers, I think you said, were Chabadnics? Were they?

A Yes. Not professors. They were -- yes, rabbis, at the yeshiva.

Jacobs-cross-Hellerstein

Q   Did they at any time speak of having come into this library and spent time researching?
A   They were not research scholars. To my knowledge, they never did research or were not interested in research.
Q   Have you ever met any scholar of Chabad who told you about the time he spent in this library?
A   No.
Q   Ever?
A   But then there are not many of us.
Q   Among those few who have done this, have you met anyone?
A   There are so few, if we are talking about -- we are not talking about actual Chabad Chasidim but we are talking about people who study objectively? There are so few that the ones I know use either the Bodleian British Library, the British Library, or the Hebrew University library which has a superb introduction collection, so I mean, I wouldn't suppose that it is an outstanding, the outstanding research library even for Chabad but I would imagine it is important.
Q   I think the question was, have you ever met anyone who was a student of Chabad who spent time researching in this library?

Jacobs-cross-Hellerstein

1 A   No.
2 Q   Have you ever met anyone who told you about
3 somebody else who spent time researching in this
4 particular library?
5 A   No.
6 Q   By the way, when you inspected last night the
7 library, did you have the occasion to look at the
8 secular books?
9 A   Yes.
10 Q   Would you say, it was fully a third of the
11 library?
12 A   As a rough guess, I would say at least a third.
13 Q   Were they of any unique character?
14 A   I would imagine that --
15 Q   Please don't imagine. Please tell me if you
16 know. If you don't know say you don't know.
17   THE COURT: Finish the answer. I think
18 this is a manner of expression.
19   THE WITNESS: You asked me whether --
20   THE COURT: Go ahead. Finish your
21 answer.
22   THE WITNESS: What was the question
23 again?
24 Q   Excuse me, Dr. Jacobs.
25   Were the secular books that you viewed,

Jacobs-cross-Hellerstein

in your opinion, of a unique character?

A   I was going to say, that it would seem to me that works on communism and Russian material against religion, against Chasidism would be unique.

Q   Are those kinds of materials found in other libraries?

A   Probably not. Not -- not to the extent that they are found there. I would imagine, for example, I am not sure, but somebody who is researching Chabad or Chasidism from the point of view of shall we say, the communist regime or Russian attitudes to this would find a wealth of material there.

Q   Do you know or are you imagining?

A   From the titles I would imagine. I don't really imagine. I am guessing. It seems to me that that's the kinds of library it is. Maybe it is a pity that it isn't more widely known.

Q   Have you met anyone doing studies in the relationship of Chabad or other Chasidic groups with the communist governments who has spent time researching in this library?

A   No, but I don't know that there are many people who have ever done this kind of research.

Q   The answer is no?

A   The answer is no.

Jacobs-cross-Hellerstein

1 Q   Have you met anyone who told you about someone
2 else doing this kind of a study who spent time in
3 this library?
4 A   No, no.
5 Q   When you --
6 A   Can I say, can I elaborate on what you are
7 asking me?
8 Q   I would prefer you to answer questions.
9   THE COURT: I think we'll probably get
10 through this more quickly and perhaps more to the
11 point of the issues in this litigation if you just
12 let this lawyer ask his questions, answer those. The
13 lawyer for the other side will have an opportunity to
14 examine you again and bring out any explanations that
15 he thinks are necessary.
16   Go ahead, Mr. Hellerstein.
17 EXAMINATION CONTINUES
18 BY MR. HELLERSTEIN:
19 Q   When you inspected the library, was your
20 inspection in the basement of the building, at 770
21 Eastern Parkway?
22 A   I think it was in the basement. We went
23 through one door after another. So I can't really
24 say offhand whether it was the basement. I rather
25 fancy it was but I can't say for sure.

Jacobs-cross-Hellerstein

1 Q   Kind --
2 A   I only got somewhere. After going through a
3 succession of rooms.
4 Q   Yes.
5   Were you also taken to the study on the
6 second floor that had been occupied by Rabbi Joseph
7 I. Schneersohn during his life time?
8 A   I was taken to a study. I don't know whether
9 it was that one or not.
10 Q   Was it -- was it one or two floors above the
11 library that carried the books, the bulk of the
12 books?
13 A   I think it was, yes.
14 Q   In that study, did you -- were you shown the
15 closet of manuscripts?
16 A   Closet of manuscripts?
17 Q   Yes. Were you shown such a closet?
18 A   I was shown -- I seem to recall that I was
19 shown a closet. I wasn't shown the manuscripts.
20 Q   You were not shown the manuscripts?
21 A   The manuscripts, no.
22 Q   Was your book of Ecstasy -- was your book of
23 Ecstasy something on the second Lubavitch Rebbe?
24 A   Yes. Yes.
25 Q   And if you knew that there had been a

Jacobs-cross-Hellerstein

particular manuscript by him in that closet of manuscripts, would you have been interested to read that?

A   Sure. But I've already answered that, that I had the original manuscript of the -- of that particular chap and I know who owns it now. It is somebody in London.

Q   Is that owned in private hands?

A   Private hands.

Q   Is it unusual for books of that type to be owned privately?

A   Depends by whom. This man is a professor at University College London.

Q   If there had been -- this is part of his private library?

A   I believe so, yes.

Q   I think you told Judge Sifton that you also had a library of your own?

A   Sure.

Q   And could it also be classified as your research library, as well as a general library of things that have interested you?

A   It could be. It is not totally adequate so I have to use other libraries but it could be in a way. I have used it.

577

Jacobs-cross-Hellerstein

1 Q   Could you estimate how many volumes you have?
2 A   I would say, about seven to eight thousand.
3 Q   I take it, you acquired that by using the
4 compensation that you earned as a professor and other
5 ways?
6 A   And -- and by reviewing.
7 Q   And by reviewing, yes.
8   Now, if in manuscripts the Dov Ber had
9 been edited and annotated by successive Lubavitch
10 rabbis, would you have been interested in those
11 annotations?
12 A   Not particularly, no.
13 Q   Would you not have been interested in how
14 successive rabbis of Lubavitch viewed the works of
15 their predecessors?
16 A   No. I think that would have been a hinderance
17 because as an objective scholar, anyone tries to see
18 that person while he's studying on his own and it
19 could well be a hinderance if you try to read ideas
20 or you're attempting to read ideas into him that were
21 read into him by later teachers.
22 Q   Would other scholars pursuing a discipline of
23 Chabad be interested in the way successive Lubavitch
24 rabbis interpreted the views expressed by their
25 predecessors?

A   Well, it would depend on what their field of
scholarship. If their field of scholarship was of
particular thinkers, as my field, in these two
studies, no, they would not be interested.

In fact, they would probably point in
scholarly discipline which I think asks you not to
look at this kind of material. Then they would get
confused and they would tend to read, as I have said,
other ideas into the text.

If, on the other hand, they were
interested in writing a history of the whole Chabad
movement, then surely they would be interested in
whatever has been said.

But I have never been in that particular
field.

Q   There would be others though who might pursue a
literary history of Chabad, who would look to see --
A   There might well be but I don't know of any
that got around to it. I think that it is a pity
that it is.
Q   Yes.

So a responsa from Rabbi Yehuda Leib, is
he --
A   He is one of the sons of the Tzemach Tzedek.
Q   The third?

579
Jacobs-cross-Hellerstein

1 A Yes.
2 Q If there were responsa in that closet from
3 Yehuda Leib, would that be of interest to scholars of
4 Chasidim and Chabad, in history?
5 A Yes.
6 Q With regard to various responsa, that is legal
7 commentary in the form of answer to questions put to
8 them by the various Lubavitch Rebbes, be of interest
9 to scholarship?
10 A Responsa -- you are using responsa in a --
11 Q In a technical sense?
12 A In a rather conventional way. Responsa refers
13 to legal literature usually. If you mean questions
14 addressed to the rabbis about Chasidic doctrine,
15 surely, it would be of interest to scholars.
16 Q Yes.
17   And if you -- have you read anything
18 that made reference to an inventory of manuscripts
19 kept by Joseph I Schneersohn or acquired by Rabbi
20 Joseph I. Schneersohn of such a nature?
21 A No.
22 Q You made mention of the anti-Semitic and
23 heretical books that you saw in the library, did you
24 not?
25 A Yes.

112

Jacobs-cross-Hellerstein

1 Q In your opinion, as a scholar of Chabad, would
2 those kinds of books be intended as to be accessible
3 to the Chabad community in New York?
4 A No.
5 Q Would it be, in your opinion, anathema to the
6 concepts of Chabad that such books be available for
7 admirers and adherents of Chabad?
8 A I would have thought so. That was the point I
9 made before.
10 Q So if there had been any intention to create
11 any kind of a research library open in some fashion
12 to the community, would it have been natural for you
13 to think to keep the members of the Chabad community
14 away from that library?
15 A Well, the point is, the point is that there are
16 two kinds of students of this material. There are
17 the followers of the movement, who obey the dictates
18 of the movement, obviously, because they are
19 followers of the movement.
20   And there are the objective scholars who
21 might be interested in Chinese metaphysics or might
22 be interested in Chabad metaphysics. They are
23 very few, very few and far between.
24   So that it -- my assessment of it is
25 that this library would serve a useful purpose for the

second class of students and would be anathema indeed to the first class, and I see in this remarkable liberalism on the part of the Rebbe, that there was the desire to have a research library even for the second class of student because evidently he thought this was a good thing, in spite of the fact that it would be -- it might -- it might be considered dangerous for his own followers and I cannot possibly imagine that he intended it either for himself or for his followers.

Q   So if it were not to be intended for his followers and he had a library, it would mean, would it not, that his followers could not go into that library?

A   Unless he trusted them not to look or only to look at the right kind of books.

Q   These books were not segregated, were they?

A   No. But you know, I suppose it is possible to say that a certain book which -- of which you're well aware like the essays of Ahad Ha'am, that you are not to read unless no one is looking. You know. This is -- it is hard to say, but I do find it in a way puzzling, in a way refreshing, that the Rebbe collected this kind of library.

MR. HELLERSTEIN: We might point out to

Jacobs-cross-Hellerstein

Your Honor, there are no standardizations -- I will ask the witness.

Q   Is it true there are no standardized equivalents from English into Hebrew?
A   Right.
Q   Therefore, we try to be phonetic in spelling?
A   Yes.
Q   Now, just stay with this another moment. It is not consistent, am I right, in Chabad, that one allows an adherent simply to go and trust to his own judgment what he should see and what he should not see? Usually he's told what he can see and what he can't see, is that correct?
A   I would imagine he's told in a general way. I think that mature men are given the right to exercise their own discretion in these matters.
Q   Have you been in any Chabad synagogue anywhere in the world where you saw on the shelves books that were classified as heretical or antiChabad in any way?
A   No.
Q   So is this the first library that you viewed last night where you see such books? I think you remarked that it was rather extraordinary?
A   Yes. Right.

```
                                                              583
                         Jacobs-cross-Hellerstein
 1    Q     Of Rabbi Joseph I. Schneersohn?
 2    A     Yes, yes.
 3    Q     So you wouldn't expect to see such books
 4    unsegregated in his library, would you?
 5    A     So little would I expect to find it that I
 6    could only explain it on the grounds that it is a
 7    general research library.
 8    Q     That's your inference from the fact that you
 9    observed this to be an extraordinary phenomenon?
10    A     Yes, indeed.
11    Q     Now, I take it, as a scholar of Chabad, you
12    have consulted from time to time with volumes of the
13    Igrois Koidesh, some of which are on this table?
14    A     Yes. You mean the present Rebbes -- you mean
15    the present Rebbe and the previous Rebbes?
16    Q     Yes.
17    A     Yes.
18    Q     Have you come across a letter written in the
19    spring of 1930 by Joseph I. Schneersohn to one Peretz
20    Vernik, and it has been premarked as exhibit --
21    Defendant's Exhibit 165.
22              MR. SHESTACK: May I look at it, please?
23              MR. HELLERSTEIN: Yes. Excuse me. It's
24    not in the bound volume.
25              MR. SHESTACK: I haven't seen this before
```

Jacobs-cross-Hellerstein

1 this morning, before right this moment.
2 MR. LEWIN: I received it this morning. I
3 didn't realize they would be using it with this
4 witness.
5 MR. HELLERSTEIN: Your Honor, it is not in
6 your bond volume either. If I may, I'd like to hand
7 you a copy.
8 THE COURT: Okay.
9 MR. SHESTACK: May I have a moment?
10 MR. HELLERSTEIN: What is --
11 MR. LEWIN: That's the copy of the entire
12 letter, as a matter of fact.
13 MR. SHESTACK: May I have a moment to read
14 it?
15 THE COURT: Yes.
16 MR. HELLERSTEIN: Yes.
17 (Short pause.)
18 THE COURT: All right. Are we ready?
19 MR. SHESTACK: Yes.
20 THE COURT: Go ahead. What's the
21 question?
22 EXAMINATION CONTINUES
23 BY MR. HELLERSTEIN:
24 Q   I think it's the fourth paragraph. You see
25 this phrase which I'll translate. In the translation

Jacobs-cross-Hellerstein

1 is -- in the exhibit I gave to you.
2   As I told you, my friend, I have always
3 been a collector of books. There are those who study
4 books, those who read books and those who collect
5 them. It has been my desire, therefore, to enrich my
6 library with your book and with your articles. How
7 do I go about getting copies. There are several more
8 copies, signed Joseph -- he -- several more
9 paragraphs, signed Joseph I. Schneersohn.
10   You see that?
11 A   Yes, yes, I've got it.
12   THE COURT: What's the question?
13 Q   And the question is, did you understand that
14 Joseph I. Schneersohn regarded himself as a collector
15 of books?
16 A   So it --
17   MR. SHESTACK: Excuse me. Has the witness
18 had time to read the whole letter?
19   THE WITNESS: This is just the first
20 moment I've seen this, this document.
21   THE COURT: I take it the question is
22 whether having looked at this letter, this affects
23 the opinions he's expressed?
24   MR. HELLERSTEIN: No.
25 Q   You would understand that Joseph I. Schneersohn

Jacobs-cross-Hellerstein

1 was a collector of books?
2 A   From this paragraph, not having read the
3 previous part of the letter, he's saying that he is
4 -- he says there are three kinds of -- three kinds of
5 book collectors. There are those who study books,
6 there are those who read books and I take it by that
7 he means who just read them superficially and there
8 are those who collect books. And it is my desire to
9 -- to enrich my library with your book. He's writing
10 to a rabbi presumably. Where can I buy them. Where
11 can I get them.
12 Q   Would you understand that Joseph I. Schneersohn
13 regarded himself as a collector of books?
14 A   Well, I don't know who the letter is to. It
15 seems to me this is to a rabbi because I can't
16 imagine him writing to Ahad Ha'am, saying would you
17 please send me your book.
18   What he's saying is I'm a collector of a
19 particular kind of book. Particular -- I'm a collector
20 of rabbinic books. I can't say without reading.
21 Q   Do you also see in this paragraph the reference
22 to the library as using the Hebrew word she-li
23 meaning mine?
24 A   Yes.
25 Q   That is --

Jacobs-cross-Hellerstein

1 A My library. Yes, but my library, she-li, in
2 Hebrew, doesn't necessarily mean I own it. It is not
3 a legal statement. It is my library. I assume that
4 to whom -- whom -- whoever it belonged it was his
5 library.
6 Q It does refer to something he has in his
7 possession, does it not?
8 A Well, in the sense that I -- one might say this
9 is my library, even though it doesn't actually belong
10 to me, if it is under my control.
11 The chief librarian of a public library
12 ~~may we~~ *maybe* will call it my library.
13 Q You would refer to the library of seven
14 thousand or eight thousand volumes that you have as
15 your library, would you not?
16 A Yes, I would. But I would also refer to the
17 much smaller library in my synagogue which doesn't
18 belong to me as my library because it is the one I
19 use. I have jurisdiction over it.
20 Q Rather than your synagogue's library?
21 A No, I wouldn't say rather than my synagogue's.
22 If I were in a court of the law I would say it
23 belongs to the synagogue. But if I were talking to
24 someone I would say it is my library.
25 Q It is a religious obligation, is it is not, for

an observant Jew to collect religious books, is it not? I think you mentioned this morning that the religious character of the many books in the library certainly could be expected to be a private possession?

A   Yes. I wouldn't say to collect books but to study the books.

Q   To buy books? Have books?

A   To buy books is considered meritorious, but only because otherwise one wouldn't have the books. There is no -- there is no rule in Jewish tradition which says if you can borrow a book you have to buy it. Except possibly to assist authors.

Q   Do most rabbis that you know buy books of a religious character?

A   Yes.

Q   And many buy books of a secular character as well, do they not?

A   Depends which type of rabbi, to which type of rabbi you are referring. How shall I put it? A rabbi of the old school would not buy books of a secular character.

Q   Others more westernized would?

A   Would.

Q   Yes.

Jacobs-cross-Hellerstein

1 Is it fair a statement to say that by
2 and large, rabbis are lovers of books?
3 A   Sure.
4 Q   We are all called, Jews are, the people of the
5 book?
6 A   The people of the sacred book.
7 Q   Many have extended it to the people of books in
8 general?
9 A   I can't -- I don't know of any rabbi -- of the
10 old school that would say that.
11 Q   But of the more modern school?
12 A   Yes.
13 Q   They would refer, would they not, to the books
14 that they acquired and were sitting on their shelves
15 as my books or my library, would they not?
16 A   Yes. If they bought it, it would be their
17 library.
18 Q   Is it a fact, a rather well-known fact, that
19 many of the Lubavitch Rebbes, perhaps all of them,
20 had extensive collections of their own?
21 A   I don't know of any other Rebbe who had in his
22 possession this kind of secular literature or
23 heretical literature. I don't know. I would find it
24 extremely odd to learn that they did.
25 Q   Were --

Jacobs-cross-Hellerstein

1 A   They had their own books. They had their
2 Talmud and their codes and Chasidic literature and
3 responsa literature, the kinds of things that every
4 rabbi has. Chasidic literature of course.
5 Q   There could be extensive collections of those,
6 could there not?
7 A   I don't know that I would use the word
8 collections. They were working libraries. They may
9 be very large working libraries but they were -- my
10 library is fairly large, eight thousand books. I
11 won't call it a collection. It is a working
12 library.
13 Q   All right.
14   Were you in the house next door to 770
15 Eastern Parkway, that is, the --
16 A   Yes.
17 Q   Occupied from time to time by the present
18 Lubavitch Rebbe?
19 A   I am not -- I am not familiar with the
20 geography of the place. I know I went into two
21 houses.
22 Q   Did you go into the house of the present
23 Lubavitch Rebbe, that he occupies --
24 A   I don't know where it is.
25 Q   Next door, that is said he occupies on weekends

Jacobs-cross-Hellerstein

1 and holidays?
2 A   I don't know about this.
3   THE COURT: You are asking the gentleman
4 more than he knows.
5   I take it, you went into two houses.
6 Q   Do you know of an extensive collection of books
7 maintained by the present Rebbe?
8 A   I saw some books in one of the houses, quite
9 apart from the library. It is an extensive
10 collection of books. I'm told that that's the
11 library of the synagogue. Though I am not too sure
12 about that.
13 Q   So you don't really know?
14 A   I don't know. I went into two houses. One was
15 770. The other was some other number. It was either
16 772 or 768.
17 Q   Have you heard it said that the present
18 collection of the present Lubavitch Rebbe is about 50
19 thousand volumes?
20 A   I haven't heard it, but I take your word for
21 it.
22 Q   You don't know if you've seen it or not or its
23 character?
24 A   No. I'm pretty sure I didn't see a library of
25 50 thousand books.

Jacobs-cross-Hellerstein

MR. HELLERSTEIN: Your Honor, I just want to ask a question. I am referring to exhibits marked in the defendant's book. I would plan to offer them during my case and I just would like to show them to the witness now, without introducing them necessarily.

THE COURT: All right.

Q I would ask you to look, Dr. Jacobs, at Defendant's Exhibit 128.

(Handing to the witness.)

A Yes. Yes, I have seen this. I have seen this document.

Q Incidentally, you mentioned that you had reviewed all of the plaintiff's exhibits. Did you also review all of the defendant's exhibits?

A No.

Q The --

A But I have seen some of them. I have seen this one.

Q All right.

Now, this is a -- an extract of a will, is it not?

A Yes.

Q And it is the will of one of the Lubavitch Rebbes, is it not?

Jacobs-cross-Hellerstein

A   Yes. The one -- two before this one.
Q   So it would be the fifth?
A   The fifth.
Q   And there are references to various annotations of that including annotations by the present Lubavitch Rebbe?
A   Yes.
Q   The first paragraph makes reference to all his books except for those itemized which he leaves as an inheritance to his son, long may he live. His son was Joseph Isaac, was he not?
A   Yes.
Q   And do you know approximately how many books Joseph Isaac inherited from his father?
A   No.
Q   Or the character of those books?
A   I would be very surprised to find that they were -- they were -- any of the type of literature to which I have referred, namely, heretical or anti-Semetic or communist literature.

I would imagine that they're all Chasidic books. He -- it says Chasidic books and mentions by name.

I would imagine these are books that every rabbi would have and he may have had a very large collection of responsa, for example, but they're all works of study.

The point I want to stress is, what -- of course there are rabbis who have more bread and butter. They would have more than perhaps the Talmud and the codes. They might have scores of responsa literature because they are students of the Torah and the Torah is as wide as possible.

But that is very different from what we understand today as research. Research is the -- refers to the objective, the objective study of the material in a "scientific" way, scientific in quotes. That is to say, one sits down before the facts like a little child and one doesn't know where it is going to lead. If you have that kind of approach, you can't prescribe beforehand the kind of books you're going to have and you certainly can't say I'm not going to look at these books because they're heretical. Therefore there are two kinds of libraries.

That's what I mean by research library. It is not so much the difference in size. You can have an old fashioned library that is -- has many volumes. You could have a research library that has few. It is not so much the size as the aim or

Jacobs-cross-Hellerstein

purpose of the library.

It seems to me that if you have a library which contains history and the -- and the kind of intervention, it -- it could hardly be the kind of traditional rabbinic library and it is a library for modern scholars, who may not be Jews at all and who may indeed be antireligious but they happen to be studying this aspect of Judaism, or that aspects of Judaism and --

THE COURT: Mr. Jacobs, let me just interrupt.

I have a feeling you think Mr. Hellerstein keeps asking these questions because he has not understood what you have said before. I don't think that's why he's asking these questions.

Just listen to --

MR. SHESTACK: I had the same impression, Your Honor.

THE COURT: All right. Go ahead.

I think Mr. Hellerstein probably understands very well what you've said.

Go ahead.

Q   This was an incident of inheritance, was it not?

A   Yes.

Jacobs-cross-Hellerstein

1 Q The books being passed down by inheritance from
2 father to son?
3 A Yes.
4 Q And from father to three grand daughters?
5 A Yes. Yes.
6 Q And there are specific references to certain
7 particularly Chasidic books that he is giving to his
8 daughters?
9 A Yes.
10 Q For their -- his grand daughters for their use
11 and their husbands' use?
12 A Yes. He doesn't say their use and their
13 husbands' use. He says they are given -- they are
14 given to the grand daughters obviously in order they
15 may give these to their husbands for study.
16 Q Yes.
17 He also disposes of various cash he
18 has? And properties, does he not?
19 A Yes.
20 Q At the bottom paragraph of the translation,
21 there are references to gold and silver dishes, funds
22 and household items?
23 A Yes.
24 Q Gold coins? Snuff boxes? Gold and enameled?
25 A Yes.

                                                              597
                        Jacobs-cross-Hellerstein

1   Q   Chanukah lamps?
2   A   Yes.
3   Q   Those are --
4   A   I wouldn't say snuff boxes. Gold and enamel
5   snuff box. I take it that means a stuff box that's
6   made of gold and enamel.
7   Q   Do these suggest to you a certain scope of
8   richness?
9   A   To answer that, one would have to know richness
10 is a relative term. What did other people in
11 Lubavitch have at that time?
12 Q   What is --
13 A   The fact the man has a gold and enamel snuff
14 box wouldn't necessarily make him a rich man.
15 Q   What period of time are we talking about? When
16 did the --
17 A   We are talking about -- if I -- he died in the
18 20s, didn't he? I believe.
19 Q   Right. He died before the revolution, did he
20 not?
21 A   In the 20s?
22 A   Did he die before the revolution?
23 Q   Thereabouts?
24 A   Thereabouts.
25 Q   It is not critical exactly when.

Jacobs-cross-Hellerstein

1 What was the condition of Russian Jewery
2 at the time? Was it rather poor?
3 A   Poor, yes.
4 Q   Rather dark, probably, was it not?
5 A   I would say so.
6 Q   Does it suggest to you by this enumeration of
7 specific items that there was a certain scope of
8 wealth to the rabbi?
9 A   Well, it probably means that he lived better
10 than the average of his followers. I wouldn't say
11 there is anything in here which suggests great
12 wealth.
13 Q   All right. We go on --
14   THE COURT: Mr. Hellerstein, what's the
15 number of this exhibit?
16   MR. HELLERSTEIN: Yes. The number is 128,
17 Your Honor.
18   THE COURT: Go ahead.
19 Q   And he goes on, does he thought, in his will to
20 make mention of three parcels of real property, house
21 in Lubavitch, a mansion in Vitebsk, and a mansion
22 with a yard in Rostov?
23 A   Yes.
24 Q   Does the -- the mention of three parcels of
25 real property of this nature suggest a certain scope

Jacobs-cross-Hellerstein

of wealth?

A   I suppose they do, yes.

Q   I think you mentioned that there was no particular virtue in Chabad to be wealthy but would it be fair to say it was no sin either?

A   Sure. Sure.

Q   The --

A   But may I say that the point I was trying to make was that in certain other versions of Chasidism, wealth is not mutual, as far as the Rebbe is concerned. The Rebbe had to be a wealthy man and supported by his followers to be wealthy. This I don't find in Chabad. The fact that a Chabad Rebbe may be wealthy is no contradiction to what I have said.

Q   No. There is nothing wrong in being wealthy?

A   These were not Franciscan Monks. They didn't make a virtue of poverty.

Q   Does looking at this will suggest that there was a rather considerable scope of wealth to this particular Rebbe?

A   Yes. But my further point was since there is no particular virtue in richness, the Rebbe, the Rebbe who was wealthy, Chabad Rebbe who was wealthy presumably got his wealth from other means than using the maamad of his followers because this would seem to me to be quite abhorrent, granted the Chabad philosophy.

Q   What other source of wealth, Rabbi?

A   It is known, for example, some Rebbes -- and I am not speaking only of Chabad, some Rebbes were sort of sleeping partners in the business affairs of their followers. Some people, some Rebbes would even give advice to their followers in business deals and they would then get a share of the profits.

There are various ways. Some may have won lottery tickets because they didn't believe there was anything wrong in taking lottery tickets, so there were various ways.

But this is a very different thing from saying that the Rebbe should be a rich, a rich man at the expense of his followers. This is only possible in a trend of Chasidism which feels that there is a mystical significance to the wealth of the Rebbe because he draws down the channel of grace and therefore he's giving more than he's receiving. I don't find this in Chabad.

Q   You say that this wealth described in this will was uncharacteristic of Lubavitch Rebbes?

A   Well, I know that the Alter Rebbe, the founder

                                                           601
                    Jacobs-cross-Hellerstein
1   of the movement wasn't a rich man and the Mittler
2   Rebbe certainly wasn't a rich man.
3   Q   But you say the fourth Lubavitch Rebbe, was he
4   a rich man?
5   A   The fourth Lubavitch Rebbe, I believe was a
6   rich man.
7   Q   And the fifth?
8   A   The fifth is the one we are talking about?
9   Q   Yes.
10 A   I don't know about the fifth. The Maharash,
11 the fourth one is known to have been a wealthy man.
12 There is no evidence whatsoever -- it seems to me it
13 would be quite contrary to the philosophy of the
14 Chabad he was rich because of donations of his
15 followers because of the maamad.
16 Q   In your studies, have you come across any
17 source for the wealth of the fifth Rebbe? Other than
18 maamad?
19 A   No.
20   (Continued on next page.)

Jacobs-cross/Hellerstein

Q   In your studies have you come across the source of the funds of the Fourth Rebbe other than maamad?

A   I am sorry, I didn't -- I don't see that there is anything here to suggest that the Fifth Rebbe was a terribly wealthy man. The answer is no.

But, then, I do know that Rebbes apart from Chabad managed to acquire a certain degree of affluence without requiring to be supported by the maamadot.

My point is that this was done. For example, members of Chernoble dynasty were wealthy because their followers supported them and gave them money for the reasons I gave.

But this seems to me to be completely contrary to the philosophy of Chabad in which the grasping ego is considered to be an evil and it is inconceivable that the leader of the movement would be so indifferent to this as to acquire wealth at the expense of his followers.

Q   Do you know the Russian word "pood"?

A   I have heard of it.

Q   Is it like 40 pounds, the Russian weight, he said.

Jacobs-cross/Hellerstein

1 A   I am pretty sure it is the same word as pound
2 but I don't know what it weighed.
3 Q   There has been testimony by Hanna Gourary one
4 of the three daughters of Joseph I. Schneersohn
5 that before the communist regime confiscated their
6 house in Lubavitch there were hanging lamps,
7 Persian carpets and a Chanukah lamp of 18 pood of
8 solid silver.
9   Would you consider that uncharacteristic
10 of the Lubavitch Rebbes to have that kind of
11 wealth?
12 A   It is impossible to answer this.
13   If we are talking of wealth we are
14 talking about a relative thing. One would have to
15 know how many of his followers had two Chanukah
16 lamps and what 20 pood of silver would be. It is
17 impossible to answer that.
18   But there is no evidence -- let me put
19 it to you this way: The Chasidim are expected to
20 cater to the needs, to see that the Rebbe's needs
21 are catered to. That's obvious.
22   When you are talking about needs needed
23 to be catered to, it is a relative term. One man's
24 needs are not another man's needs.
25   Who is to decide what has man needs?

Obviously for Chasidim it would be the Rebbe. The Rebbe has to decide.

So, if the Rebbe decides it is necessary for his needs to function as a Rebbe that he has to have a silver candelabra for Chanukah, so, obviously, that is part of his personal needs and he does it. And no one chances to exercise control and says no, that you don't deserve this. It would be absurd.

But the Rebbe by the same token would exercise discretion in this matter.

I gave the illustration with one of the other groups, they would ride in a carriage with four white horses, exactly as a prince, a Polish prince or count.

So, they were putting themselves on a par with the aristocracy.

Q They want to display their wealth?

A Yes. Because they believed there was virtue in this.

This is not there in Chabad, and Chabad would be opposed to it. It is opposed to their philosophy.

What does one do? One leaves it to the discretion of the Rebbe how many pounds one menorah

Jacobs-cross/Hellerstein

1 weighs or how many tapestries one should have.
2 Q   It is fair to say that the Rebbe doesn't
3 account for the money given to him, is that
4 correct?
5 A   Yes.
6 Q   He gives no one an accounting how he spends
7 his money? He could send it to Israel to support
8 scholars, spend it on his house? Give it to a
9 scholar in a local yeshiva?
10   THE COURT: Mr. Hellerstein, please.
11 These are not questions. Let's get answers from
12 the area that the witness is an expert in.
13 Q   Would it be consistent with your
14 understanding of Chabad philosophy for a Rebbe to
15 be able to spend his money on all of these kinds of
16 activities and for his own household without
17 accounting to anyone?
18 A   Yes.
19 Q   I would like you now to look at Exhibit 108,
20 which I would now hand to you, Defendant's Exhibit
21 108?
22 A   Yes.
23 Q   This is a document that has been excerpted
24 from the Igrois Koidesh and also produced in full
25 text as a manuscript from the closet of the study

Jacobs-cross/Hellerstein

1 of Joseph I. Schneersohn?
2 A   I am familiar with this.
3 Q   You are, good.
4   Let me, again, use the English
5 translation, and refer you to the --
6   MR. SHESTACK: May I just note, your
7 Honor, that this has not been offered as an
8 exhibit. We do not accept that translation as an
9 accurate translation.
10   THE COURT: Let's see if we can work
11 with it just as a basis for examining an expert.
12   MR. HELLERSTEIN: I represent to your
13 Honor that this --
14   THE COURT: I really don't need to go
15 much further into it. An expert can be examined on
16 matters not in evidence and base his opinion on
17 matters not in evidence.
18   What is the question you wish to ask?
19 Q   Is this as you understand it, a letter, from
20 the fifth Lubavitcher Rebbe, Sholom Dov Ber
21 Schneersohn?
22 A   Yes.
23 Q   And is it a letter to Rabbi Yitzchok Chaim
24 Dov Ber Wolenski, a luminary of the time?
25 A   Yes. The word "Wolenski" doesn't occur, but

Jacobs-cross/Hellerstein

I am told it is. In the text it just says Dov Ber, not Wilenski.

Q And is this a letter which makes inquiry as to legal obligation on the part of the Lubavitch Rebbe to brothers and sisters on account of an inheritance from the fourth Lubavitch Rebbe?

A Yes.

Q And does it make reference to a property, to property that was distributed to the brothers and sisters?

A Yes.

Q And does it make reference to an exchange by the fifth Lubavitch Rebbe of manuscripts coming down from his predecessors in exchange for his share of some of the material possessions which were distributed to the brothers and sisters?

A Yes.

MR. SHESTACK: I object to the characterization of the letter. It is a series of what Mr. Hellerstein thinks is in the letter.

THE COURT: I will take these as assumptions which I believe the witness is prepared to make with respect to the contents of the letter. As to whether this is what the letter says or not, why not wait until the time it is offered

                    Jacobs-cross/Hellerstein

1   in evidence, if it is offered.
2   MR. HELLERSTEIN: It will be, your
3   Honor.
4   THE COURT: Assuming that this is what
5   the letter is about, what do you want to know from
6   the witness?
7   MR. HELLERSTEIN: Does this letter make
8   reference to considerable wealth which was
9   distributed by the Fourth Lubavitch Rebbe, by the
10   brothers and sisters to the Fifth Lubavitcher
11   Rebbe?
12   A   Yes.
13   Q   Make reference to a soap factory?
14   A   Yes.
15   Q   And lumber fields?
16   A   Yes.
17   Q   Considerable loans?
18   A   Yes.
19   Q   Retail department store operation?
20   A   Yes.
21   Q   In major Russian cities?
22   A   Yes.
23   (Whereupon, there was a pause in the
24   proceedings.)
25   THE COURT: While you are looking for

Jacobs-cross/Hellerstein

something, let me ask you, in the original, what is the word that is translated here, I think it is on page six, as sacred works in the phrase, if I may, therefore, take the sacred works as my share of the inheritance?

THE WITNESS: Page six?

THE COURT: Yes.

The fifth line from the top there is a reference to sacred works. I am really asking whether that is an accurate translation. And if so, to what in your opinion that that refers.

THE WITNESS: Sacred works.

Can I look at the original?

THE WITNESS: Yes, please.

(Whereupon, there was a pause in the proceedings.)

MR. HELLERSTEIN: There is a transliteration attached, your Honor, that may make it easier.

THE WITNESS: This, you mean?

It is very difficult to read the original document.

"Sifrei Kodesh" -- I am almost whether sure the Hebrew is "sifrei Kodesh", which means holy books.

Jacobs-cross/Hellerstein

1 THE COURT: What sort of works would
2 that be?
3 THE WITNESS: Religious books, Talmud,
4 codes, Responsa and that type of Chasidic
5 literature.
6 MR. SHESTACK: May I ask who did the
7 translation of that particular exhibit?
8 MR. COGAN: Mr. Leiman.
9 MR. HELLERSTEIN: The translator that
10 both sides used, your Honor.
11 MR. SHESTACK: What is the Hebrew of the
12 word that was used?
13 THE COURT: When it is offered, if it is
14 offered, you may make suitable inquiry.
15 Anything more from the witness on this
16 subject or any other subject?
17 MR. HELLERSTEIN: Yes, your Honor.
18 Q Close to the close of Mr. Shestack's
19 examination and the first part of my
20 cross-examination we made reference to the letter
21 in 1946 by Joseph I. Schneersohn to Alexander
22 Marx.
23 What were the conditions in Poland at
24 the time as far as you understood it, as they
25 applied to Polish Jewry?

Jacobs-cross/Hellerstein

1 A   It was after the war?
2 Q   Yes.
3 A   My impression from the letter is if the State
4 Department, the American State Department, were
5 urged to do something about it they would be able
6 to recover the books.
7 Q   Were the conditions in Poland rather chaotic
8 as they applied to Jewry?
9 A   Yes.
10 Q   And those Jews that had survived the
11 Holocaust and returned to their hometowns in Poland
12 after the end of World War II, were they subjected
13 to pogroms?
14 A   I am not an historian.
15 Q   As far as you remember reading the press at
16 the time, Doctor Jacobs, is it a fair statement?
17 A   I can't answer. It was a long time ago.
18 Q   Was the Government in Poland friendly to
19 Jews?
20 A   I don't think so.
21 Q   It was a communist government at the time,
22 was it not?
23 A   Yes.
24 Q   And was there a time when --
25   MR. SHESTACK: Excuse me, your Honor. I

Jacobs-cross/Hellerstein

tried to get into that, and Mr. Hellerstein said that he is not qualified. I don't mind Mr. Hellerstein getting into it, but I would be expected to redirect on that.

THE COURT: It seems to me that this is beyond the scope as to why the witness was brought here. I am sure that there are other people who would be able to to testify on this subject.

Is there anything more?

MR. HELLERSTEIN: Yes, your Honor.

(Whereupon, there was a pause in the proceedings.)

Q This morning you were asked in connection with a discussion on maamad to look at Exhibit 45, Plaintiff's Exhibit 45.

If you don't mind, I will put this in front of you.

(Handed to the witness.)

Q Are there two purposes for maamad as it is explained in the first paragraph of this document?

A Yes.

Q And one is to help the present Rebbe in his household; is that right?

A I did mention this.

The Hebrew is "le'bais chayenu". It

Jacobs-cross/Hellerstein

certainly doesn't mean in his household. It would seem to be in opposition, namely, to the Rebbe, namely, Bais Chayenu.

Q   And how would you understand Bais Chayenu? As court? I think that's the way you said you understand it?

A   Yes.

Q   Everything about where the Rebbe lived?

A   If you are stressing the word "ba'yit", I would say no. It is just a term, "bais chayenu". It doesn't refer to the physical house.

Q   The second part of it goes on to say according to the interpretation, for the general efforts.

Would you look at the Hebrew?

A   "Bi'shvil avoda ha'klalit", yes.

Q   "Bi'shvil" means for?

A   Yes, avodat ha'klalit.

Q   Is that a "vav" at the end?

A   Yes.

Q   What does that mean?

A   His work, his general work.

Q   So, we are talking, are we not, maamad for the Rebbe's Bais Chayenu or the general work for the Rebbe, are we not?

A   The general activity, not work for the
activity.

Q   Activity?

A   Of the Rebbe.

Q   So, the first part is for the Bais Chayenu of
the Rebbe?

A   I wouldn't say that. "Le'bait chayenu" is a
technical term for the Rebbe. Because elsewhere
you have Bais Chayenu, may he live long.

I would interpret this to mean to help
the Rebbe, the Rebbe and his court.

Q   Number one?

A   Number one. And for the general purposes for
which he uses it.

Q   Number two.

A   But general purposes the word "avodat" to is
used here and that would mean his religious
purposes. It is Avoda. It didn't mean for any
purpose for which he wishes.

Q   In the second part?

A   In the second part, yes.

Q   Okay.

I think you mentioned you remembered an
earlier antecedents of maamad at the time of the
temple in the offerings that were made by the

Jacobs-cross/Hellerstein

1 levites and the priests.
2 A   Not quite.
3   There were three people who stood by the
4 sacrifice in the time of temple, three categories,
5 one the priests, the second the levites and the
6 third is the men of the maamad, who were groups of
7 people who came from time to time who represented
8 the rest of the Jewish community in Palestine.
9 Q   And they ministered?
10 A   They were simply there. It was considered
11 then as everyone being present at the time the
12 sacrifice was offered.
13 Q   And who consumed the sacrifice? The levites
14 and the priests?
15 A   The levites, no.
16   Sometimes -- some were consumed by the
17 priests and some were consumed by the people who
18 brought it.
19   It so happens that the maamad were there
20 for the perpetual offering which was offered
21 morning and evening. And this was a burnt offering
22 so no one consumed it. It was consumed on the
23 alter, but they had to be present as
24 representatives of the community.
25 Q   And other offers were given to the levites

Jacobs-cross/Hellerstein

and priests for their consumption?

A   Not given to the levites. Some were given to the priests and some given to the people who brought them. Peace offerings.

Q   You mentioned "pidyon", I think, as an offering to the rabbi made in person for a blessing or some other act of kindness on the part of the Rebbe or intercession with God?

A   Yes.

Q   And in the modern western world where Chasidim have departed from their community in the in the eastern world and now spread around the world, is maamad the way Chasidim link themselves to the Rebbe?

A   If you are asking is maamad a substitute for pidyon, the answer is no.

Q   No. I am not asking that.

How, in tangible expression can a Lubavitch Chasid link himself to the Rebbe if he is away from the Rebbe? Is that by maamad?

A   Yes, maamad.

Q   And this giving of maamad to the Rebbe is an acknowledged way in which a Lubavitch Chasid links himself to the Rebbe, is it not?

A   I wouldn't put it quite that way. I would

Jacobs-cross/Hellerstein

say he links himself to the Rebbe by giving the maamad. One function is to support the Rebbe, but it has other functions as well.

Q   Yes, of course.

But is it a function of the Agudas Chabad or other organization that were developed by Lubavitch to link and group the Chasidim in the ways of linking themselves to the Rebbe?

A   Yes.

Q   I think you said that there can be no such thing as a Chasid without his Rebbe?

A   Yes.

Q   And is this fraternal organization or set of organization that were created, and the maamad that passes through them, a way that the Chasidim links themselves to the Rebbe?

A   Links themselves to the Rebbe, but the Rebbe being the major part of the community. But it is a communal thing.

It is true that you can't have a Chasid without your Rebbe. But you can't have a Rebbe without Chasidim.

So, it is a fraternal thing.

Q   Yes.

But does that fraternal body not pass on

```
                                                          618
              Jacobs-cross/Hellerstein
```

1 at least a portion of the maamad to the Rebbe? Is
2 that not one of its functions?
3 A   Yes, it does pass on.
4 Q   And as I understand it, and tell me if it is
5 true, the Rebbe gives no accounting of what he does
6 with that money, does he?
7 A   As well as I know he doesn't.
8 Q   Yes.
9 A   Or he is not expected to.
10 Q   And I think you have written in your essay
11 that found its way to the Encyclopedia Judaica,
12 that the Rebbe, and it is true of the Lubavitch
13 Rebbe, is an absolute authority and interprets the
14 world to the Chasidim?
15 A   I think so.
16 Q   And to interpret the world to the Chasidim he
17 must have a profound understanding of the world?
18 A   No.
19   I am not saying he doesn't have a
20 profound understanding of the world. But in
21 interpreting the world simply means interpreting to
22 the Chasidim man's role in life, what the purpose
23 of existence is, why do we exist, what are we
24 living for. He doesn't have to have knowledge of
25 the world for that.

Jacobs-cross/Hellerstein

Q And in the western world and the confusion of modern objects, automobiles, theater and all kinds of things, is it not one of the functions that Lubavitch Rebbes have taken upon themselves to filter the experiences of the modern world so that the Chasidim could understand it and keep to their faith?

A When you mention theater, surely Lubavitch uses drama and things of that kind and television.

But, theater, some of the books in the library are Yiddish plays, plays performed in the Yiddish theater.

I can't in my wildest dreams imagine a Lubavitcher Rebbe going to a Yiddish theater to watch a particular play or to. be at all interested in it.

Q Would it be fair to say that if a Lubavitch Rebbe took upon himself the obligation to understand what is going on in the modern world and all its ramifications so he could be a better leader to his Chasidim, could that not be a consistent aspect of the way he perceives his role?

A If the Rebbe did this it would be accepted by the Chasidim. But I would find it a very unusual thing for the Rebbe to do.

Jacobs-cross/Hellerstein

Q You would?

A I would.

And I mean judging by the little knowledge I have of how rebbes operate.

Q If Joseph I. Schneersohn through his library and through activity with others took it upon himself to understand the nature of the heretical writings and antisemetic writings so he could be a better leader for the Chasidim, would you find it inconsistent with his role as a Rebbe?

A If he, shall we say, wanted to read, to give the example that I gave, to read the essays of a Ahad Ha'am, in order to familiarize himself with attacks on Chasidim, sure, it is possible. I don't think he did it. It is not my impression that he did it. But it is possible that he did it.

Then he would buy a cheap copy of some of the letters of Ahad Ha'am or read a book on Ahad Ha'am or study it in a spare moment so to know what to do when confronted with the modern world.

He certainly wouldn't have a collection of that kind of material. There is no time for anyone, let alone a busy Rebbe, to read that kind of material for any length of time.

So, the only purpose would be to have a

Jacobs-cross/Hellerstein

1 research library for people who want to study that
2 kind of period or that kind of thinking.
3 Q   How would you know that never having made a
4 study of the life of Joseph I. Schneersohn?
5 A   How would I know?
6 Q   Yes.
7 A   How would I know that Reb Yossef Schneersohn
8 would not have gone to the Yiddish theater?
9   I wouldn't know him personally and if I
10 did I wouldn't be with him all the time. And it is
11 quite possibly that he could slip off when no one
12 is watching to go and watch a Yiddish play.
13   I think it is so unlikely and anyone
14 whoever thought about it would say it is extremely
15 unlikely.
16   So, we can say with confidence that it
17 didn't happen.
18 Q   Perhaps if it was unlikely that he slipped
19 off to see a Yiddish play could he not substitute
20 the printed wording of the play from his library so
21 he could read it on a Shabbes afternoon?
22 A   I would say it is extremely unlikely, contrary
23 to anything I know of Chasidim.
24 Q   Is it fair to say that you yourself are a
25 controversial figure in English Jewry?

Jacobs-cross/Hellerstein

1 A   I suppose you could say that.
2 Q   Is it fair to say that the chief rabbi at the
3 time, Doctor Brody, he blocked your appointment to
4 Jews College in Oxford?
5 A   Jews College is in London.
6 Q   I am sorry, where was it you were seeking
7 appointment?
8 A   Yes. Jews College in London.
9 Q   And he blocked your appointment?
10 A   Well, it is a complicated story, but roughly
11 speaking you could put it that way.
12 Q   And when you wanted to return to your
13 synagogue on the west end of London, did he not
14 block your return to that pulpit?
15 A   Yes, yes.
16 Q   And are you familiar with a book edited by
17 Menachem Mark Kellner entitled Contemporary Jewish
18 Ethics?
19 A   Yes. Two essays of mine are in the book.
20 Q   Is there also a critique of you --
21 A   Yes. By Sid Leiman, L E I M A N, associate
22 professor of Yiddish studies at Yale University.
23 A   Yes.
24 Q   May I read his comments. More disturbing is
25 the methodology Jacobs employs in arriving at his

Jacobs-cross/Hellerstein

conclusions by means of a highly selective choice and interpretation of materials Jacobs has imposed his view on the classical texts with the process he may have raised more problems than he solved, close quote.

Do you consider that a fair critique?

A   No.   I think he is wrong.

Don't yourself be guilty of selective quotation because Leiman says at the beginning that I am something like the best writer on Jewish ethics writing today.

MR. HELLERSTEIN: Thank you, Doctor Jacobs.

THE COURT: Do you have any other questions of the witness?

MR. LEWIN: If your Honor would maybe take a three minute recess I will abbreviate my questions by going over the ones that I had written down.

THE COURT: We will do that.

(Whereupon, a recess is taken.)

MR. SHESTACK: Thank you, your Honor.

Jacobs-cross/Hellerstein

REDIRECT EXAMINATION
BY MR. SHESTACK:
Q You had previously referred to an appointment that had been blocked in England by the chief rabbi, but counsel didn't ask you why it was blocked.

Would you tell us why.
A In so far as I could make out, it was because of my acceptance of the findings of modern biblical criticism.
Q In other words, you were not quite fundamentalist enough?
A Yes.
Q And you were not blocked because of any lack of expertise on Chabad philosophy, were you?
A No.

Nor was I blocked because of any lack of ability in scholarship. It is quite the opposite. This was really the issue, whether free objective scholarship is permissible within the bounds of traditional Judaism.
Q Mr. Hellerstein asked you about some of the use in some of the Igrot, letters, of the word "sheli", "sifriya sheli", which was translated by him or you as "my library".

Jacobs-cross/Hellerstein

Do you find any examples in the Igrot of the Rebbe using the words "yeshivot sheli"?

And if you do, would you please explain what that means?

A   Yes.

The Rebbe here in a letter dated -- it doesn't have a date, but it is from New York. It is Simchat Torah, actually --

MR. HELLERSTEIN: May I object, your Honor? I don't know what exhibit number we are referring to.

THE WITNESS: It is the letters of Rabbi Joseph Yitzchok, number 210, page 94 -- 96 to 97, wherein he talks about, he says: I am thanking you, one and all, for your gifts and for taking a part in the work of help and rescue in order to rescue the students of my yeshiva in Europe, the students of my yeshiva, my yeshivot.

Q   He uses the Hebrew word "yeshivot"?

A   "Yeshivot sheli". It didn't obviously mean that he owns the yeshiva or owns the bnai ha'yeshivot.

Similarly, on page 213 he says again, referring to the same theme, he says to help them, to help support my yeshivot in Lithuania and Latvia

```
                   Jacobs-cross/Hellerstein
 1    and Palestine, in Eretz Yisroel.
 2    Q    He wasn't in your opinion referring to the
 3    yeshivot as his personal property?
 4    A    Well, how could he?
 5    Q    There is an exhibit called the Wolfenski
 6    letter which has been identified by
 7    Mr. Hellerstein. And in it there is a reference to
 8    sacred books.
 9         Do you know what the correct Hebrew is
10    as to that?
11    A    Yes.
12         His Honor asked as to that. And I
13    couldn't decipher the actual writing. I thought it
14    was Sifrei Kodesh, or holy books. Actually it is
15    Kitvei Kodesh, and "Kitvei Kodesh" means
16    manuscripts.
17    Q    Not books?
18    A    Not books.
19    Q    Thank you.
20         From time to time in connection with
21    maamad, the words "Bais Chayenu", "the house of our
22    life" was used and explained. And there is also
23    the use of the word "anash".
24         Can explain what that means?
25    A    Anash is an abreviation for "anshei
```

Jacobs-cross/Hellerstein

familiarity with research libraries and other great libraries.

Q Have you seen in his writings any reference to such libraries?

A Yes.

There is a document in which he wishes to have catalogues. There are great American Jewish libraries.

And he mentions, as I recollect, the library of the Jewish Theological Seminary, the library of the Hebrew Jewish College and the New York Public Library and others.

This can only mean to me that he was concerned to put together a respectable research library analogous to those three and to the others.

And then the question would be, why should he do a thing like that?

It seems to me the only possible thing could be for prestige reasons.

Even though it basically goes against his philosophy to have those books that I mentioned, have books that are irrelevant to any purpose like long series and periodicals and consequently he had it, it seems to me. And a way to explain it is to bring prestige.

Jacobs-cross/Hellerstein

1 Q To whom?
2 A Then the question would be to bring prestige
3 to whom?
4   And it could either be to the movement
5 or the Rebbe himself.
6   To my mind it is quite inconceivable
7 that a Rebbe at the expense of his followers should
8 collect large amounts of money and use it to
9 collect a library solely for his own prestige. And
10 it can only mean it is for the prestige of the
11 movement.
12   He thought evidently that it would be a
13 good thing if Lubavitch has a library analogous to
14 the other great libraries.
15   Whether it is run as well as the other
16 great libraries, and if that's the question that is
17 put to me, is really irrelevant.
18   Maybe if it was run by persons better
19 known more scholars would use it. But it doesn't
20 affect the nature of the library or the intention
21 of the Rebbe.
22 Q Doctor Jacobs, Mr. Hellerstein referred to a
23 book called: Contemporary Jewish Ethics, to a
24 critique of you in that in chapter three by Sid L.
25 Leiman.

```
                                                          630
                      Jacobs-cross/Hellerstein
 1            I would like to read the first paragraph
 2    of that which reads as follows:  Clearly, the most
 3    articulate Jewish essayist in recent years has been
 4    Louis Jacobs, whose ethical concerns have found
 5    expression in the numerous books and theologies,
 6    studies and scholarly editions of classical texts
 7    he has edited and published.
 8            Are you that Louis Jacobs?
 9    A     I am, presumably, yes.
10            MR. SHCSTACK:  Thank you.
11            No further questions.
12            THE COURT:  If there is nothing more?
13            Thank you very much.  And you are
14    excused.
15            (The witness is excused.)
16            THE COURT:  Are you prepared to resume
17    with the testimony of the witness who was on the
18    stand previously.
19            MR. LEWIN:  Yes.
20            We will continue with Rabbi Krinsky.
21            We had another witness whom I mention to
22    Mr. Hellerstein whom I hoped to testify, he has
23    already lost two days work.  And I decided since we
24    will be adjourning in another hour and a quarter to
25    be able to get him in.  We will call him again to
```

Printed in Great Britain
by Amazon